A BRILLIANT
TV WRITER/PRODUCER

ARNOLD KANE

ISBN: 978-1-09831-874-1 (print)
ISBN: 978-1-09831-875-8 (ebook)

Contents

A DEDICATION:

To Murray and Betty Kane – my parents.

To all those men and women who have passed during my fifty years in show business. Some were friends, others just enter- tainers I work with. If I tried to list all of them it would look like the Yellow pages so here are just some:

Mike Stokey, Anne Francis, Mary Tyler Moore, Mike Douglas, Bruce Johnson, Bill D'Angelo, Antonino Rocca, Pat Summerall, Sam Denoff, Sonny Grosso, Frank Brill, Jack Benny, George Burns, Alan Rafkin, Dixie Carter, Bernie Brillstein, Pat Harrington Jr., Harvey Korman, Bonnie Franklin, Ray Allen, Jim Nabors, Werner Von Braun, Leo Durocher, Skip Steloff, Sonny Bono, Earle Hagen, Leonard Goldberg, and recently Saul Turtletaub.

HOW IT ALL STARTED:

I am often asked how I got started in the Entertainment Business. Coming from a long line of sheep herders there seems no obvious connection between the two careers. Growing up in New York City it became apparent that Manhattan didn't offer me much of a chance to make a living in the family business. You might not realize it but sheep herding – except for a few areas of Soho – isn't exactly a growth industry in the Big Apple. What to do? I decided to look for another career that didn't take many brains, creativity, or talent – hence I chose to devote my life to Producing and Writing.

AUTHOR'S NOTE:

In that I set out to defame and vilify many of the actors, writ-ers, directors, studio and network executives I've worked with – my hot shot attorney suggested I use caution in naming names. When talking about some pain in the ass he suggested I cover- up their true identity. For instance, when talking about Linda Lavin, the star of the series "*ALICE*" – rather than use her actual name I disguise it by saying, "The star of *ALICE* who shall remain name-less." (Pretty darn clever if you ask me). No wonder I pay him huge bucks. Most of the unprofessional and insecure types I write about bear no resemblance to anyone living or dead. There's an old Flemish curse: "I hope you inherit a hotel with one million rooms and are found dead in each one." That would be too good for many of these nudniks.

Did you know if you stick your tongue in someone's ear when they're making a speech, they will immediately begin to sound like the late Jerry Lewis doing his 'monkey character'? That thought has nothing to do with my personal and professional life – I just think it's funny. "Funny" has everything to do with my life. It's how I earned a living for over fifty years. Thinking funny and trying to be funny was also how I tried to live my personal life. I pity my loved ones and friends having to deal with a real- life Bozo the Clown. Now that my body is sagging a little and my memory isn't…uh…isn't…see, I forgot what I was going to say. I don't want to talk about my liver spots. I hate liver spots! The only way I want to see liver is on a plate with mashed potatoes, sau- téed onions, and lots of ketchup. Well anyway, I thought it was time to sit down and relate some of my experiences – both good and bad, some funny, some sad, about my life in Television and the people I worked with over those fifty years.

This is not a 'how-to-book'. If I knew 'how to', I'd still be working instead of waiting for the two--dollar residual check from the "*The Jefferson's*". I still think I'm as funny as anyone working in TV, but no one gives a crap about some gray-haired guy with liver spots. I've had a pretty wonderful time during the years I produced and wrote some television series. My career spanned LIVE television to multi-cameras, video tape, instant re-plays, and digital editing. Most of it was a blast. I was fortunate with some of the biggest stars in Show Business. Many were dolls – few were putzes. I also got to know lots of Studio and Network bosses. Some creative, most dumb as shit. I earned a damned good living during those fifty years. No regrets. Since this is my book my praise and gratitude might embarrass some of my friends and co-workers, but they'll get over it. If some of the peo- ple think I was too rough or made them out to be monsters – so be it. They'll get over it, too. I consider myself lucky to have worked in the entertainment business all my adult life. Can't think of anything I would rather have done. Carl Reiner once said to me, "Do you know how lucky we are? We come in every morning, sit at our typewriters (guess how long ago that was) and make funny faces and noises and get money at the end of the week." The man was right.

I hope you enjoy the read.….

CHAPTER ONE

THE BEGINNING

AS MUCH AS I'D LIKE TO SAY "I WAS BORN IN A TRUNK at the Prin- cess Theater in Pocatello, Idaho" as Judy Garland sung in a movie – I wasn't. The Brooklyn Jewish Hospital gets that dubious distinction. Ours was a normal dysfunctional family. My father Murray was a wholesale florist and my mother Betty was a stay at home mom. I had an older brother George who I'm sure barely put up with his younger, nervous, pain in the ass brother. My par- ents seemed reasonably content with each other. I don't remem- ber much touching, hugging, or the family standing around sing- ing Welsh mining songs.

What I do remember was that we had one of the first TV sets in the neighborhood. It was a 9-inch black and white Dumont. I would stare every free moment, since programming was restricted to a few hours a night. I mostly watched the TV Test Pattern.

Didn't matter to me…it was still magic. Maybe deep down I knew or hoped that one day I would work in this new me- dium. I gotta say that those Test Patterns were more entertaining than most of the Network shows today. Our entire family loved to go to Broadway musicals. We'd buy the 78rpm albums and listen to them all day. I knew the lyrics to every song from every musical on Broadway. I think it was these experiences that formed my lifelong love affairs for musicals. When I got older, I even auditioned for a few. More about that later.

Brooklyn was a great place to grow up during the thirties, forties, and fifties. It had wonderful neighborhoods, friendly people, and safe streets. We also had the Brooklyn Dodgers! God, they were fabulous – even if they were in last place. Ebbets field was the most exciting place in the world to watch baseball. It was a small, intimate ballpark which attracted the wildest, most bizarre fans in the country. *"One Flew Over the Cuckoo's Nest"* had nothing on a typical crowd at Ebbets Field. There was *Hilda Chester,* a female baritone and her cowbell and *Gladys Gooding* the ballpark organist, who when the UMPIRES took the field used to play *THREE BLIND MICE.* And of course, *RED BARBER,* the voice of the Dodgers.

There was also a famous sign on the right field wall publicizing Abe Stark's Men's Shop. If any batter hit the sign, he won a free suit. The only problem was the sign was 4-feet off the ground and the right fielder stood directly in front of it. I don't think Abe ever had to give away a free suit. Years later he became the Mayor of NYC. My father and his partner knew the Dodger manager Leo Durocher, so we had a box at all the games. As a kid I was often taken into the clubhouse to visit "Uncle Leo". In the mid sixties

I wrote and produced a TV series call Magic Moments in Sports and Durocher was the narrator. He remembered me sitting on his lap in the Dodger dressing room. Fortunately, I didn't have to sit on his lap during Magic Moments.

I was a pretty awful student in school. I failed *Kindergarten*. Never liked school and didn't apply myself during grade, high school, and college. My teachers claimed my I.Q. was the same as my neck size. Later in life, some friends swore that the film "DUMB & DUMBER" was based on my school years. While at Long Island University – the only college in America that would accept me (that's the truth) – I got involved in their Theater program and found I had some talent in that area. I was a lousy actor, but I had balls and was never afraid to try. I learned about hanging lights, painting, and building scenery, and being a stage manager. I was like a sponge when it came to learning the tech- nical aspects of putting a show on. That experience came in handy when I began producing Television series.

CHAPTER TWO

"DO YOU ALWAYS HAVE TO BE SO FUNNY?"

"DO YOU ALWAYS HAVE TO BE SO FUNNY?" I ACTUALLY heard the late Jerry Lewis' wife complain about that during a Comedians golf tournament. What the hell did she think he did for a living, sell shrouds?

While still a student at L.I.U., I began to perform as a stand-up comedian. I played small clubs, dances, and even a few dates in the Catskills in New York. Trust me, Jack Benny and BuddHackett had nothing to fear. Something every comedian needed to be was funny (if not, the audience can get very hostile) and an act. And most importantly was a tuxedo. In those years, no self-respecting comic would ever step on the stage without a tux. Today, an audience is lucky if today's so-called comedians wear underwear. The tuxedo era didn't change until the Chicago group of comedians burst on the scene. People like Bob Newhart, Nichols & May, Mort Saul, Shelly Berman, etc.

Instead of 'rim-shots' these performers did character comedy. They talk about 'real' people and real problems. To go along with their new comedy, they dressed informally and killed their audiences. Tuxedo manufacturers went into mourning when the business changed. Poor Henny Youngman never knew what hit him. I loved the feeling of standing in front of an audience and getting them to laugh. All those years as the class clown came in handy. If you didn't know who the President of the United States was you'd do a 'spit-take'. Spit-takes is where you pretended to be shocked and sprayed your drink all over the place from your mouth after hearing something *that took you by surprise*. It was usually good for a cheap laugh. My material was either stolen from established comics, or I'd try to write stuff myself. Who knew that I'd spend fifty years doing it successfully? Stealing material was an honorable profession in those days. In the fifties, there were big charity benefits every week in places like Madison Square Garden. Every great comic would do a turn. Other wan- nabes and I would stand backstage trying to be inconspicuous and listen to them. I would also whisper jokes and lines that I liked into a hidden tape recorder. I wasn't the only young guy doing it.

My experiences as a would-be comic were fabulous. The feeling you have standing on a stage and 'playing' an audience is powerful. The excitement knowing that a laugh was going to happen just as you planned it was gratifying. When you didn't get the expectant laugh, it became 'panic-city' time. You felt as pop- ular as a leper and about as talented. If you've never experienced "flop-sweat" do yourself a favor and don't. As soon as the first 'sure-fire' guaranteed joke bombed, your stomach dropped like you were free-falling from a jet at twenty thousand feet with no parachute. You begin to perspire in places you never knew you had. Your knees began to knock and you'd find yourself speaking like one of those chipmunks in those comedy records.

Of course, while all this is happening you could never let the audience know you were close to hysteria. Even if you were the newest and rawest comic in town, there was a brotherhood (now sisterhood, also) of fellow comedians who would welcome you with open arms. Comedians generally like each other. They like to hang out together. They want you to do well, but not as well as they're doing.

You can't learn to be funny! You're either born funny or not. Yes, you can learn technique and stage presence, but no one can teach you how to look at the world in a comedian's slightly off-beat, cockeyed way. Most comics use their humor as a de- fense mech- anism. It's easier to make a joke than face and emo- tionally deal with a tragedy. That's one of the reasons after some- thing horrible happens fifty great jokes spring up.

It's no accident that most comedians are from ethnic mi- nori- ties. Comedy was a way for them to get back at people op- pressing them. If you gave a finger comically to the folks running things you could get away with it without being boiled in hot oil. That tradition goes back to Court Jesters. It's one of the reasons that so many comics are Jewish, Irish, Italian, Black, Latino, and Women. I've never heard of a comedian from Switzerland or Ice- land. What the hell do they have to complain about?

To illustrate it even further – in 1974 we were all saddened to hear that comedian Harvey Stone had died. Harvey had ap- peared on the Ed Sullivan Show as many times as any comic with the exception to the great Senor Wences. Harvey was one of the kindest and nicest guys in the business, but like many co- medians of that era didn't like to change his material. "If it ain't broke why fix it?" The trouble with Harvey's material was it was BROKE. He was still doing his routine about getting in the Army during World War 2. Still doing the material twenty years after the war was over. Audiences didn't want to hear the same old act. I know because I tried to write new stuff for my friend Harvey, but he resisted changing his material. He was married to a former dancer who was very beautiful, bright, and tough as nails. She had become Harvey's manager. Anyway, night clubs began clos- ing all across the country because of free television. Getting jobs was more diffi- cult if your act was considered dated and old fash- ioned. Harvey took a gig on one of those cruise ships in the Car- ibbean at the time of his death. Jobs were scarce and comics took any job they could get in those days even if you hated the water, which Harvey did. During the cruise he had a massive heart attack and died. The ship's Captain called Harvey's wife in New York with the terrible news. The Captain was very solicitous and said they could do one of three things with Harvey's body. They could keep him in cold storage until the ship got back to New York. They could unload his body when they reached the next port and arrange for him to be shipped home…which could cost quite a bit of money – or they could bury him at sea. What!? Harvey Stone was a guy who got seasick in the shower. Without taking a beat his wife told the Captain that Harvey always wanted to be buried at sea. "That Harvey always wanted to be buried with the nice fish." Obviously she didn't want to be bothered with any expenses and funeral.

When everyone at the Friars Club heard what happened – a roar went up. Gales of laughter mixed with outrage. The thought that poor sweet Harvey Stone's face as he hit the water probably saying, "Good evening Ladies and Gentlemen…what the FUCK!"

I know it's strange to say, but comedy is a serious busi- ness. Off-stage, many comics are unhappy, neurotic individuals, but when they get on stage, they blossom. The best comedy is based on adversity, jeopardy, and fear. It's the difference be- tween an episode of "The Honeymooners" and "Leave it to Bea- ver". There was <u>always</u> something at stake between Ralph and Alice on the Honeymooners. The Beavers may have been a cute kid but nothing really important ever happened on that show. This rule holds true for stand-up comedy as well as TV sitcoms. It's easier to be funny if you're talking about a subject that pisses you off or is important to you. Something I learned early on in my performing career is that stand-up comics are aggressive on stage. A lot of comedy is based on anger, hence the phrase that a performer "killed the audience" – "I murdered them". A come- dian challenges an audience. They dare them <u>not</u> to laugh. A great comic's seeming self-confidence will always win out. After telling a joke the late Bob Hope would just stare at the audience until he got his laugh. It didn't matter how long he had to wait, he'd wait and eventually get his laugh. He was a master at it. Jack Benny's famous hand on his chin waiting almost told the audience that they should laugh now.

When I started out as a young comic no one used "blue mate- rial". It was a no-no. Not even contemplated. A dirty per- former would be barred from clubs or stages. Most comedians were story-tellers. They had routines which were written for them or in a few cases they wrote themselves. The comics perfected them by performing them over and over. Their audiences could also relate to what they were complaining about such as: mar- riage, kids, in-laws, bosses, taxes, sex, politicians, loss of hair, airlines, etc., etc. Too many comics today think that all they have to do is stand-up, curse, and do racial jokes in order to shock their audience into a response. Their comedy isn't about any- thing; it's just a series of vulgar words. I wish kids today ap- proached their humor and acts more intelligently. They just go out and say "Fuck" a lot. Sadly, it seems to work.

The funniest thing that ever happened to me as a wannabe comic was on a club date in the Catskills. For any of you who don't have the foggiest about the Catskills, it was to perform- ing as the Vatican is to Catholicism. Even if you didn't headline at Grossinger's or the Concord hotels. They were the big-time per- formers and could still play two or three club dates a night in small hotels or bungalow colonies. Most bungalow colonies clientele were Jewish. They were often Orthodox Jews not known for their rollicking humor. The wives and kids would stay in the country all week and the husbands come up for the weekend. The Orthodox bungalow colonies had one thing in common – every family shared the same large communal kitchen. They also paid the tal- ent very poorly which is why you'd do two or three club dates a night.

Anyway, this one Friday night the 'show' drove up together. We saved money that way and everybody chipped in for gaso- line. Doesn't sound very glamorous, does it? It wasn't. The 'show' consisted of a dance team, a Black singer and of course me – the comic/MC. I forget the name of this particular joint as they all looked alike. We arrived and checked out the 'show room'. At this colony the 'show room' was a large, uneven lawn in the middle of the grounds. It had no stage…just bumpy, rocky grass. A huge old spotlight was focused on a standing mic. That was it. We all mumbled, "oh, shit!" We were not even working indoors. We could be attacked by locusts. But hey, it was show biz.

The people began to gather on the lawn, bringing wooden folding chairs from their bungalows. They unfolded their chairs, sat down and waited to be entertained. Showtime! I ran out, stood in front of the mic and realized I was in big trouble. They had put the mic under a large tree branch which hung down about face level. I had to hold the tree limb up with one hand as I talked to the audience. Thank God I wasn't a juggler. Lifting the limb from in front of my face, I told the crowd how happy I was to be there. Someone coughed. I said what a great crowd they were. The truth was I couldn't see two inches in front of my face. The monstrous spotlight was blinding me. I introduced the dance team Pedro & Olga who tried to do their act but kept tripping on the grass and rocks. It wasn't a pretty picture. They were lucky to escape without broken ankles. After some applause that sounded like a fart, I introduced the singer. He sang some stand- ards and after about 15 minutes he finished with "*MY YID- DISHER MOMMA*". The crowd went wild. In the Catskills, every smart black entertainer did something Yiddish in their act. If this guy had decided to make chicken soup on stage he would have headlined at the Concord and been elected Prime Minister of Is- rael. The comic/MC was always the headliner and was expected to do at least a half an hour of material. Let me be honest – I wasn't that great a comic anyway but still holding the damn tree limb up I began my act. I was lousy and getting silence from the crowd. I figured I'd better do my top material and started to hear some claps. Then more claps and more claps. I was getting to them. I finished my act, but instead of a standing ovation there was dead silence. Somebody turned off the spotlight and the lawn was empty. No people. What I thought was loud clapping were the sounds of the folding chairs being noisily folded up as the people disgustedly went back to their cabins. I had cleared the joint out. I had laid a bomb bigger than all the bombs we dropped in Baghdad.

I never did find out if I could have made it as a full-time comedian. Two things made me decide to try other areas of Show Business. The first was when I got an audition with the booker for Tamiment. It was a hotel that put together a group of young performers and writers every summer that would do origi- nal material and shows every week. One night it might be a variety show, the next an original play, etc., etc. It was a world- famous training ground for some of the best performers to ever step on a stage. Needless to say, I was very excited and thrilled with the opportunity. My brother, George, by this time became an agent for the William Morris Agency. They unofficially repre- sented me as a comic and arranged for the audition. When the time came for the audition, George offered to come with me. I happily accepted. The booker was in a dingy office building just off Broadway. His office was furnished in early Bail Bond. It was decorated with a wooden desk with cigar burns all over it and a threadbare carpet.

After a little schmoozing, he told me to stand in front of his desk and do my act. That was it. He was sitting behind his desk about ten feet away and my brother was sitting behind me. Pretty glamorous, heh? If I did well, I would be hired for Tamiment that summer. My act took about thirty-five minutes. I was about two minutes into the act when his phone rang. The booker put up his hand to stop me and took the call. After five minutes he told me to continue. I picked up where I left off and after a minute or two the lousy phone rang again. This went on for the rest of the au- dition. I started speaking faster hoping to get more material in before his phone rang again. I must have sounded like a speeded-up record. My thirty-five minutes turned into twelve minutes of double talk. The booker thanked me and told George that he'd let the Morris Agency know. We left the building and I felt like walking into the traffic. I was convinced that I'd never work at the hotel except as a waiter. I was sure my career was over – that I was a failure.

Imagine my surprise when a few weeks later I learned that the booker had liked me and that I was booked into Tamiment as the second banana to Don Adams. Maxwell Smart, this! I was floating on air. I couldn't wait to get up there. This meant I was really in Show Business. About 4 days before I was to leave for the hotel, I got a call un-booking me. They had gotten a comedian with a little more experience. My big break was over before it began. Needless to say, I was very depressed and began to question whether I really wanted to spend my life as a comedian if this is what I had to look forward to.

The nail in my comedy coffin was struck by Danny Simon. Danny was the older brother of Neil Simon and a famous comedy writer. Danny and Neil wrote for Sid Caesar for years and had won many Emmy Awards. They were both comedy legends. Neil decided he wanted to just write plays and Danny figured he'd look for a young comic whom he could groom and write for. The Morris office arranged a meeting for me with Danny Simon. At the appointed time I was sitting in an agent's office. When Danny arrived, he took one look at me and announced that "he's not funny looking. He'll never make it." Without another word, he walked out. I'm not making this up. It happened. I don't know what Danny Simon expected. Maybe some guy in a clown suit and a putty nose. That's when I decided I didn't have the stomach or guts to be a comedian. I became a good friend of Danny's later on. In fact, he wrote a couple of scripts for me when I moved out to California and became a TV producer.

"THE TV BUSINESS IS A CRUEL AND SHALLOW MONEY TRENCH – A LONG PLASTIC HALLWAY WHERE THEIVES AND PIMPS RUN FREE AND GOOD MEN DIE LIKE DOGS!"

HUNTER S. THOMPSON

CHAPTER THREE

TV AND ME

IN 1956 I HAD GRADUATED FROM LONG ISLAND University and was wondering what I was going to do with my life when I re- ceived a phone call which changed everything. It was from the William Morris Agency and they had a job for me. Mike Stokey's TV game show "*PANTOMIME QUIZ*" was moving to New York as the summer replacement show for the interview show *Person to Person* on CBS." *Pantomime Quiz,* at the time, was the long- est running television program on air…it had been on for ten or twelve years always originating from California. The program was a charade game played by some fairly popular Hollywood actors. Mike Stokey was the host – in fact, he won the first Emmy ever given for that kind of show. The performers all wore tuxedos and gowns. They would make fools of themselves playing cha- rades. It was funny and I remember watching it for years.

Stokey was offered the Person to Person time slot and grabbed it. J. Walter Thompson owned the time slot and Life Magazine was the sponsor. In the fifties, sponsors were the power and networks had little to say as to programming. The net- works simply broadcast the shows. Pantomime Quiz was or- dered for ten shows with a built in Person to Person audience and was expected to do well. Stokey was coming to New York to change the look of the show and breathe a little life into it. No more tuxedos. It had become a bit stuffy. He was looking for a young guy who knew the comedy talent in town and to help write the 'stumpers' – the charades. The Morris Office recommended me to him – we met and liked each other, and I got the job. I was paid the grand salary of $200.00 a week. Today, that's less than unemployment insurance but in 1956 it was huge money for a snot nosed kid. Frankly, I would have signed a pact with the devil if I could have guaranteed two-hundred bucks a week for the rest of my life. No one questioned my qualifications. If Stokey thought I could do the job, that was good enough for everyone. Network interference didn't exist in those glorious days. Not until the sev- enties did networks decide that they knew how to do the job bet- ter than the creators and that they knew who should be hired with their approval. We have Fred Silverman to thank for that disaster. He was heading up CBS and was convinced he was smarter than anyone else. Silverman changed Television for the worst his en- tire career.

Since Mike didn't know NYC comedians or young performers, he allowed me to basically book the show. Among them were: Dick Van Dyke, Carol Burnett, Robert Morse, Merv Griffin,

Howie Morris, etc., etc. A few standbys like Hans Conried and Peter Donald were also booked. Mike and my job in writing the 'stumpers' was to allow the performers to show their physical tal- ents off. Van Dyke was always given a very physical charade because he was brilliant doing them. Our viewing audiences ac- tually thought the charades were sent in by the audience, but they were written by us. Mike was very generous in teaching me how to produce and I'm grateful to him to this day…even though he's in the great charade in the sky. We did the show "Live" in those days. Video tape hadn't been invented yet. The only neg- ative in doing Pantomime Quiz that first year was being exposed to the TV blacklist. Yes, "The Red Scare", when Americans were terrified if international communism was alive and well in 1956. Senator Joe McCarthy was still a powerful influence especially with spon- sors. The threat of their products being removed from the super- market shelves or boycotted by customers, panicked ad agencies as well as huge corporations. It seems like a fairy- tale today, but it was pretty scary and devastating to the poor actors who were being blacklisted and their lives ruined by those right-wing crack- pots. Many actors committed suicide when faced with the reality of never working again. Many were completely innocent and a few admitted to being communist. Very few. I was given a phone number by J. Walter Thompson to call whenever I wanted to book a performer. The rule was that I gave that per- former's name and then I would be given permission, or not.

As a very, young liberal man, those orders didn't sit well with me, but it was made very clear that I had no choice in the matter. Here's how it would work – just say I wanted to book…say… Johnny Carson on the program – I would call this mysterious, unlisted number and a faceless voice would say, "yes." I'd tell him who I was, and what the show was that I wanted to book Johnny Carson. There would be a pause as this Nazi looked through his files and would finally agree to Carson's ap- pearance. The first time I was told, "No!" was when I wanted to book Robert Clary. Clary had just starred in "New Faces" on Broadway. Clary later went on to star as Louis LeBeau in Ho- gan's Heroes. Clary was an adorable little Frenchman who spent his childhood in a German Concentration Camp. He still had a goddamn tattoo on his fore- arm. After what seemed like an hour, 'the voice' came back on the line and said "NO" and hung up. Thinking we were disconnected, I called back. "Hey, we were disconnected. I was trying to book Robert Clary and…" The voice cut me off, said "NO!" and hung up again. I was furious and called back and insisted on knowing why I couldn't book Clary? I started to yell, "Don't you realize that Bob Clary survived a concentration camp, and still had a tattoo on his arm…" The voice just hung up on me. About five minutes later Stokey came out of his office ashen faced. J. Walter Thompson has just called him and sternly told him that unless 'his staff' behaved and stopped causing problems, they would cancel Pantomime Quiz. That was my first experience with the Black List. Thank God those days are over. Or, are they?????

We did ten shows and they were big hits. I was now an official television producer. Stokey was coming back the next summer for thirteen shows and asked me to join him again. I happily agreed. The problem with producing just ten shows was that I was unemployed for the rest of the year. I earned two-thou- sand dollars. There were no game or comedy programs looking for a new producer. I lived on unemployment insurance of thirty- five bucks a week and waited until the following summer. Work- ing only a few weeks a year didn't bother me, in those days. Firstly, I was living at home with my parents and when I finally moved out it's amazing how nicely you could live in a rent con- trolled apartment and have thirty-five dollars burning a hole in your pocket then. Later on of course when I wasn't working, de- pression would rear its ugly head and I would go into a large de- bilitation funk. Sadly, that way of life became a huge problem for my entire adulthood.

One of the perks of the job was that I got to be good friends with Dick Van Dyke and Carol Burnett. We used to hang out dur- ing the rest of the year because none of us were that busy work- ing. Dick got a job on NBC radio and he and I would meet for drinks, get bombed, and then he'd hop a train for Long Island. There was no indication then that he had a problem with alcohol. Years later he joined AA after some serious booze related incidents. Carol was living in a cold-water flat in Hell's Kitchen with her first husband Don. Carol and I would meet for coffee and Danish – I paid, of course since I was a big time TV producer. Dick and Carol are two of the nicest and most talented people I ever met in the business.

My life as a summer replacement producer continued for another three years. Finally, in 1959, Mike called to tell me that ABC had bought the show as a daytime strip – meaning we were to do five shows a week during the day and in addition they ordered one nighttime program…making a total of six Pantomime Quiz's a week for an entire season. This was big time stuff. Oh, by the way, since I'm a business idiot, he told me he was still going to pay me $200.00 a week. I didn't tell him to stuff it – I agreed.

It's obvious that I would have been a candidate to Donald Trump University. The word SCHMUCK fits me real well! In spite of all that, we had a ball doing the 1959 season. I was allowed to hire a real staff as well as to use new performers since we were doing so many shows. Carol and Dick joined us once again. It was during that season that year that Carol was spotted on Pan- tomime Quiz by Mary Rodgers, daughter of Richard Rodgers and author on "*ONCE UPON A MATTRESS*". Mary Rodgers hired Carol to star in her musical. I had read a biography of Fanny Brice, a famous vaudeville and radio comedian. The book was called "*THE FABULOUS FANNY*". I instantly knew that I wanted to do it with Carol Burnett playing Brice. My idea was to do it as a TV Special and I began negotiating for the rights to the book. I made Carol read the book and she agreed with me. She loved it. Carol got all teary-eyed and told me she totally identified with Fanny. Both thought of themselves as ugly ducklings and had problems finding a good man in their lives. Carol insisted I call her manager and discuss it with him.

Like most managers, he found reasons why she shouldn't or couldn't do it. What it got down to was a lack of imagination on his part. Throughout my career, I have found that it's easier for agents and managers to say 'no' to projects. That way their asses are never on the line. Oh, by the way, a Broadway musical opened a few years later on Broadway. Perhaps you may have heard of it. It was "*FUNNY GIRL*", the Fannie Brice story. It made Barbra Streisand a mega star.

Burnett was a smash hit in Mattress, first off-Broadway, then on B'way. Gary Moore who was a huge TV star went to see Carol one night and immediately hired Burnett for his hit TV se- ries.

The rest they say is history. The next year Dick Van Dyke starred in "BYE-BYE-BIRDIE" on Broadway and soon after had his own brilliant television series, "THE DICK VAN DYKE SHOW" with Mary Tyler Moore. It's pretty amazing what an influence a silly charade game had on both their lives.

Because "Pantomime Quiz" was on the air so much with our six show a week schedule, it suddenly had value to certain people. They were 'product placement' folks. Their job was to get products seen or mentioned on the air which was publicity for merchandise. Most of these dudes were pretty shady. They usu- ally had a glint in their eyes reminiscent of a claim jumper in an old Republic western film. Stokey was thrilled with them since he received CASH every time a product was shown or mentioned on his show. We had two guys who handled PQ and they would call me and say, "if we had one of our cast holding a Coke bottle, Mike would make this much money." It was the earliest form of payola. One day they called and asked if I could get the Benefi- cial Finance Company into one of the charades? I laughed and told them to get a lobot- omy. How the hell could I slip Beneficial into a charade without getting arrested?

Never take a product placement *gonif* lightly. One of the guests on that show was the old comedian George Jessel. George showed up wearing a powder blue tuxedo and asked me to have Mike ask him about it. Mike and I figured that George had a funny story about the tux – so on the air – Mike asked, "George that's some tuxedo. Where did you get it?" Without missing a beat George said, "The Beneficial Finance Company." The pricks had gotten to Jessel and he took their cash. Mike Stokey was pissed. Another perk was the clothing deal I was able to get for Mike.

The manufacturer would give Mike five free suits a week for a wardrobe credit at the end of each program. This perk still goes on today. Look for it on any TV series you watch. Over the 1959 season, Mike must have gotten a few hundred free suits. He gave some freebies to ABC executives in charge of the show. They were on the take, also.

That year we did the series from ABC's 'Little Theater' right next to Sardi's Restaurant. It was a great, small intimate theater and allowed me to book a lot of stars from Broadway shows run- ning near us. PQ wasn't the only series coming from the Little Theater that year. Some of the others were: *"WHO DO YOU TRUST"* starring Johnny Carson – that was way before the To- night years and Dick Clark's *"SATURDAY BAND-STAND SHOW"*. We all became friendly and kibitzed a lot. Carson was going through one of his divorces and would often sleep in his office. I was always the first person to arrive at the theater each morning and if I saw the lock to the stage entrance gate cut in half, I knew that Johnny had gotten bombed the night before, taken some bimbo up to his office/pad and then hadn't been able to get her out after they did 'the dirty'. He would call ABC security and they'd drive over and cut the chain and lock in order to let Johnny's 'date' out.

One night during a PQ taping – Carson wandered onto our stage drunk out of his brains and holding a large Hebrew National Salami. Our live audience was surprised and applauded like wild. Johnny began to do 'suggestive' things with the salami and Dick Van Dyke who was on our panel grabbed Carson…pulled him down next to him and averted a potential disaster. When Johnny's agent heard about it the next morning he called me and sounded like someone had thrown him off the Empire State build- ing. He begged me to burn the tape or Johnny's career was over. What tape? We did our shows LIVE. Fortunately, things quieted down but they owed Van Dyke big time.

I've been asked through the years whether I ever had the cliché 'casting couch' in all the years I've been in the business. The answer is a resounding, "Hell, No!" It never occurred to me to take advantage of women – especially on my office couch. I was fortunate having my own chair. To try and seduce someone by using my power as a producer was not my way of thinking. I was too serious about my job and I had too much respect for the performers. It just seemed so tacky! However, the same didn't hold for many executives at ABC in 1959. I can't tell you how many times those guys would call and 'need a favor.' I helped them if I could – I was working at their network.

Toward the end of the '59 season all hell broke loose in Television. The Quiz show scandals had just made headlines and the D.A.'s office decided to question every daytime and nighttime game or quiz show producer to discuss "irregularities". PQ's problem was that Mike Stokey got greedy. We were doing six shows a week using lots of charades for which prizes were supposed to be given to the people who sent in the cha- rade/stumpers. Since Mike and I were writing them all we would make up names of people and towns and the 'prizes' would really be sent to a warehouse that Mike had rented. If the authorities found out about this scam, Mike would be in BIG trouble and his career would be over. I didn't think I'd get into any trouble since I never received any of the prizes and I was happy getting my lousy two-hundred dollars a week. To play it safe I decided to take a 'vacation' with my childhood friend and associ- ate producer David Fein. David had served in El Paso, Texas while in the Army so we headed down south. From there we took a train to Hollywood where I visited Anne Francis. I don't think Stokey was ever called by the D.A. but interestingly PQ never aired on any network again. It was four interesting years in which I learned my craft.

CHAPTER FOUR

TONY SOPRANO
IS A WUSS!

IN THE LATE FIFTIES I MET ONE OF THE MOST INTER-
esting guys I've ever known. He was an attorney named Frank
Barone. Besides being a fine lawyer, Frank was the manager in
those days of the popular singer and recording star Julius La Rosa.
Frank also car- ried a big gun in a shoulder holster. This was years
before The Godfather, so all I knew about the mob came from
movies and watching the Television series The Untouchables. I
had never met anyone before who packed a gun. I became a favorite of Frank's especially when I bought him a shoulder holster I
got in Mexico for Christmas. He told me it was the nicest gift a
client had ever given him. Barone was a very dignified, low key
gentle- man who obviously was well connected with strong men
whose names ended in vowels. Capish?

Through Frank I was introduced to a small Italian restau- rant on West 46th Street called The Amalfi. It was a tiny place with unbelievable food. The window in front was covered by drapes so that passersby's couldn't look in. In hindsight it was probably used to stop any bullets that might have been fired from the street. Most of the Amalfi patrons didn't like strangers watch- ing them eat – especially cops. The owner's name was JIMMY. He was a huge bear of a man who could have bench pressed a truck. Jimmy took a liking to me and I would eat there two or three nights a week. The other clienteles usually consisted of elderly gentleman whose rings got kissed a lot as well as bodyguards with no necks and muscles in places I didn't even have. Since Frank Barone had vouched for me was welcomed by every pinky ring. The first time he took me to Amalfi, Frank had firmly told me I was always to be a gentleman in the restaurant and to never, never ask anyone for a favor. After hearing that, I was afraid to ask a waiter for a glass of water! Now this was years before...Don Corleone – so I wasn't sure exactly what he meant, but I agreed to what he said. Some nights when I had eaten someplace else I would knock on the Amalfi door around 10pm – the joint closed very early – Jimmy would peek out from behind the curtains, see it was me and unlock the door to let me in for a nightcap. He would usher me to the small bar and pour me a drink. A few of the tables were always crowded with some guys with bulges un- der their jackets. Obviously they knew I was harmless and would continue their whispered conver- sations. For all I knew many hits might have been being planned and I was an unknown witness.

It was during this time that I met actress Anne Francis and we became an item whenever she was in town. Anne was one of the most beautiful women I ever saw in my life. She had a sexy mole/ beauty mark on her cheek that drove me crazy. In fact I nicknamed her "the mole" which I called her until she passed away a few years ago. When Anne came to New York City to publicize a movie she had just done, I would book her on Panto- mime Quiz. She was a pretty well-know movie star and I would often bring her to the Amalfi for dinner. Jimmy fell in love with Anne and would look forward to her visits. If she was in town and I didn't bring her in Jimmy would growl and give me a look that would cause a Yak to have a heart attack.

One night Anne was invited to a party at Sammy Davis Jr.'s suite at the Warwick hotel. Sammy was starring on Broadway in "Golden Boy". Apparently every celebrity in town was at the party. The next morning Anne called me in a panic and crying at my PQ office. This is the story she told me...as she left the party Sammy saw her to the hall, they kissed each other on their cheeks and a flashbulb went off. She didn't think anything of it. Earlier that morning a photographer who worked for CBS and moonlighted at Confidential Magazine which was the leading rag at the time took a picture of the kiss. He called Anne and threat- ened to give it to Confidential unless Anne had sex with him. In those days a black and white actor's careers could easily be ru- ined by that kind of picture. She was petrified and didn't know what to do. She was sure her movie life was in the dumper that she would never work again. I told her to calm down that I would handle it and call her back. Remember, I was a big time TV pro- ducer earning two-hundred a week. I really didn't have the faint- est idea how to help, but ignoring Frank Barone's warning I called the Amalfi.

Jimmy answered the phone and I told him Annie had a problem. He began to grind his teeth.

When I finished telling him the whole story he quietly said everything would be taken 'care of' and not for Anne or me to worry. About three hours later Anne called and said she had just gotten off the phone from a crying, hysterical Dave H. (the photographer) begging Anne not to let the two thugs standing next to him kill him. Jimmy had obviously made a call to two killers, wearing pinky rings as big as hubcaps who went to CBS and Dave's office there and told the poor guy that he was "a dead nigger" and after he gave them the negative of the photo they were planning on taking him to the Hudson River to see how good he could swim with cement fins on his feet. They were not joking. When Dave called Annie he was blubbering and pleading for his life. Anne told the goons that she didn't want Dave hurt she just wanted the picture destroyed. The bulvans must have checked with Jimmy and here's what they worked out. Dave H. was told to leave NYC and not to return for five years. If he did he would be killed on sight. The guy left town that day and never returned. Anne couldn't thank Jimmy enough for taking care of her problem. He told us both it was his pleasure and to come in for dinner on him.

When Frank Barone found out what I had done he went bananas! He screamed at me, "I told you never to ask for a favor, didn't I?" I answered, "Yes, Frank." Barone snarled, "Schmuck, now you owe them and if they ever need a favor from you, you've got to do it." I smiled, "Frank, what kind of favor could Jimmy as me to do?" He stared back and seriously said, "You don't want to know." Until I read "The Godfather" I didn't know what he was driving at. A few Years later I was in my apartment at London

Terrace on West 23rd Street at about 9pm and the phone rang. It was Jimmy and he was very upset and he insisted that I come down to the Amalfi...now. I did. We sat at the bar – the place was empty and Jimmy began to cry. He had received a call from Los Angeles that Anne Francis had just gotten married. His exact words were, "Why'd she do that to us, Arnie?" Oh, my God, Jimmy had fallen in love with Anne. On my way home it dawned on me – how the hell did Jimmy get my phone number? It was unlisted. The most interesting and scarifying thing I learned from this experience was how easy it would have been to have some- one killed if you knew the right people. Wow.

CHAPTER FIVE

SKIP – THE YEARS

I WAS INTRODUCED TO SKIP STELOFF IN 1960. SKIP WAS President of Heritage Productions which syndicated TV shows and was about to get into production of two new series. He asked me to write and produce those shows. Whoever it was did me a huge favor. Working with Skip was like having a New Year's Eve party every day. The guy was fabulous. He was bright, funny, balsy and totally crooked. Skip's word was never his bond. He was the kind of fella who would try to pay a restaurant bill with mattress tags. He'd say anything to make a deal or con someone. Steloff was a graduate of Annapolis and a classmate of former President Jimmy Carter's. Even at the Naval Academy Skip was known as a character.

He got his charm and unscrupulous behavior from his fa- ther, "Saratoga Ike Steloff" a legendary gambler and handicap- per.

Damon Runyon often wrote stories about Ike and his esca- pades. The one Ike liked best about himself occurred when he was a young man and decided to pull off a horse race scam with some friends. Ike had gotten hold of a pretty good racehorse – a horse that had won a few races. They took this horse up to a small track in New England. The racetrack has very ordinary horses running, none of which were ever going to get in the Ken- tucky Derby... even with a ticket. Ike registered his thoroughbred under an assumed name and made up a phony record indicating that his horse was ready for the glue factory. He and his friends painted the white spots on his horse's head and body completely brown. That way no track official might recognize his horse. Just before the race began Ike and company quickly plunked down all their money on their nag to win. The odds dropped to about 70 to 1, but it was still the longest shot in the race. The gates opened and Ike's horse went into the lead and never stopped. It was about 20 lengths ahead when suddenly it began to pour down rain really hard...down in buckets. While Ike and his friends waited for the race to end and for them to pick up their winnings. They stared in horror as the paint they had put on the horse be- gan to run off. The previously all brown horse suddenly had white spots all over its body. The jig was up. Ike didn't even wait for the race to end, he and his pals jumped into their car and beat it out of town just ahead of the police. They left the horse to fend for itself.

The apple in Skip's case didn't fall far from the tree. When Skip was growing up, he never knew from week to week whether he was going to be driven to school by a chauffeur, or the family was going to be evicted from their home. Obviously, the life of a professional gambler had its up and downs. Through his father's longtime friends, Skip got to know many Jewish mobsters like Meyer Lansky and others who would eventually own the casinos in Vegas. In fact, when I started working at Heritage Productions, Ike was running the casino at the Flamingo Hotel in Vegas. When I finally met Skip's parents, Ike and Gert, I understood where he came by his charm and spirit of fun. They were beautiful people.

The first series I did for Heritage was "GOLF TIP OF THE DAY" a series of one-hundred-fifty-six five minute shows. It starred Dow Finsterwald who was the PGA Champion in 1958. Skip's idea was to produce 5-minute shows which could be slotted into local news broadcasts, or the local stations could plug them in whenever they needed some programming. Golf Tips was the first film/location show I ever did. It was a great learning experience. It took us about one year to complete the one-hun- dred fifty-six shows. We began producing them at Englewood Country Club which was about a half hour from the George Washington Bridge. Their membership was made up mainly of show business people and some who looked liked the actors in Good Fellas.

It was a fun place to shoot and close enough to NYC for us to bring in lots of stars. Our guests on Golf Tips read like a 'who's who of the sports world and comedy business. Some of the guests were: Mickey Mantle, Roger Maris, Willy Mays, Jack Dempsey, Rocky Graziano, Joe Lewis, Frank Gifford, Dick Van Dyke, Henny Youngman, Milton Berle, Perry Como and Jackie Gleason and others. The guests had a good time and learned a little about golf from Dow. We also served a helluva lunch.

Finsterwald and I became close friends and when the win- ter weather forced us to move to the Diplomat Hotel in Florida we roomed together. Whenever we had a free afternoon Dow and I would drive to his home club in Florida and play some golf. The man would hustle me and happily take my money. We'd stay at his home and his wife Linda and his kids were very gracious to me. After we finished the series whenever Dow was playing in a golf tournament in the New York area, he would stay at my apartment. I'm proud to say that in those days I took him to the Stage Deli a lot. Dow Finsterwald never met a plate of kosher franks and beans he didn't love.

The second series I did for Heritage was "MAGIC MOMENTS IN SPORTS" with Leo Durocher. It was a film clip show featuring the greatest moments in sports history. The first opportunity I had to learn to learn about editing film. It was interesting to write since the narrative had to be timed exactly to the footage. Leo lived in Beverly Hills at the time so I would fly out to the coast to record his voice-overs. I would then fly back to Manhattan and lay his narrative into the edited programs. Leo was known as "Leo the Lip" for good reason. He was loud, opinionated, and lots of fun. I had a show about Babe Ruth and had written the line, "They had lots of names for that great, big guy." I meant, of course "The Babe", "The Sultan of Swat", etc. Durocher went crazy. He said, "Yeah, a fat drunken prick." What was that all about? I convinced Leo that calling this national icon dirty names wouldn't work on TV. I then found out that Leo played for the Yankees during his rookie season in baseball and Babe Ruth found Leo stealing his watch out of his locker. Ruth beat the shit out of Leo and the Yankees immediately traded Leo to the St. Louis Cardinals. It worked out well for Durocher when he joined the famous Gas House Gang in St. Louis and became a star shortstop. He went on to become the playing manager of the Brooklyn Dodgers and an instant celebrity. But, he never forgot his beating by Ruth and hated him for it.

It was during the production of both series that Skip Steloff said I was doing such a great job that I now owned 10% of them. I never got that promise in writing, however which was an industrial size mistake. Skip had the morals of a used car salesman. While I finished editing both series, Skip sold both series to ITC

– a very large, successful syndication company. When I casually mentioned to ITC that I owned 10% of the programs they almost fainted. But, since there was no paper there was no deal. I teased Skip for years and years about his owing me 10%. Many years later in Los Angeles I was celebrating a birthday at a fancy res- taurant when Skip entered and presented me with a check for two million dollars! There it was my 10%. It was unsigned, of course.

Despite Skip's crooked ways I loved the guy. After we fin- ished the two series, Skip's close friend Herman Rush was ap- pointed head of Television for GAC a very big talent agency. Her- man gave Skip a group of offices hoping that Skip would create a series that General Artists Corporation could sell. Herman Rush had a reputation as a brilliant salesman and businessman. I never saw that side of him. All I remember was that Herman walking around his office in bedroom slippers. One night I picked up a book called "THE LIST OF ADRIAN MESSENGER". It was a fabulous mystery. I stayed up all night reading it. The next morning, I told Skip about it and that we should buy it as it would make a great motion picture. I then got on the phone with the author's publisher and told them I was producing a television show starring mystery writers and wanted the author's phone number.

Pretty sneaky, huh? They told me the author didn't have a phone but gave me an address where I could send him a tele- gram. Skip and I created one and sent it off to Golden Gate, California. Later, when we were going to lunch, we bumped into Herman Rush in the elevator. Skip excitedly told him about Adrian Messenger and that we had to buy it. It was a potential block- buster movie. Herman took out a pad and wrote the name down and confidently told us to call him after lunch – that he would take care of every- thing. When we got back from lunch there was a telegram waiting for us from the author thanking us for our interest in his book but informing us that Kirk Douglas has just bought the screen rights. Seconds later our phone rang and it was Herman Rush. He got us the book. Skip and I looked at each other confused. "Herman, what do you mean you got us the book? We just got a telegram telling us that Kirk Douglas bought the rights." There was a pause. "What rights? I got you the book. You owe GAC five dollars and twenty-five cents. You asked me to get you the book so I bought a copy at Doubleday."

This is a true story and enough to frighten anyone. Herman may have been a genius to lots of people, but he will always be the guy who bought us a copy of a book we already had. Smart? Nah! If Skip hadn't always been looking for an edge or to out scam the world, we could have been the proud owners of "BORN FREE". We had gotten the pre-publishing manuscript from some- one and I read it in one night. The story of "ELSA", the lioness was brilliant. We got on the phone with Kenya and talked to Joy Adamson who had written the book and raised Elsa. She told us she had thousands of feet of film of Elsa as a baby and as she was growing up. The film was available to us. More importantly, Mrs.

Adamson was interested in making a deal. Instead of getting a pro to negotiate for us Skip began to low ball her until she passed on his crappy offer. She signed a deal with Columbia Pic- tures. After two successful movies and millions off the Oscar win- ning song and many millions of the merchandising, I still have nightmares at what might have been. Despite all those "coulda- wouldas" my years with working with Skip Steloff was a total joy. I wouldn't trade them in for anything. I loved the man. I guess if he were totally honest, he wouldn't have been Skip.

CHAPTER SIX

LOCAL TELEVISION AND MOI

IN THE EARLY SIXTIES NEW YORK'S WOR-TV'S CLAIM
to fame was the Joe Franklin Show. Joe's biggest claim to fame was
that he had no talent. None. Zip. Franklin had a talk/interview
show on Channel 9 for more years than anyone cares to remember.
Joe became a local joke due to his inane interviews. In fact, Woody
Allen used Joe's program on "Broadway Danny Rose". Joe's real
claim to fame was that he had an amazing collection of silent films
and would tour all over the State showing his films on a projector
and talk about the silent film era. From this humble background
he talked his way into a show of his own. You might ask why a
top-rated local station in a major market in the country would
allow Franklin to appear on the air. It was simple. He brought in

his own sponsors and that station liked that a lot. Bringing in your own sponsors was my first lesson in program- ming for local TV.

One of my oldest and best friends, David Yarnell was the program director at WOR-TV. He asked me to join the station as Executive Producer and an assistant to him. An offer I accepted gratefully. WOR-TV was the flagship station for RKO General Broadcasting a company owned by General Tire. The reality is that the only thing important to any local station are sponsors and ratings. Quality has little to do with any of the shows they put on the air. Making money was the bottom line – even if they pro- grammed to the lowest common denominator. The truth is that little has changed from the 60's in local or even network televi- sion. "Show me the money!" That's why you see so many info- mercials on local and cable networks today. They bring in pot- loads of cash. Another staple in the WOR line-up was a cooking show called "THE BONTEMPI'S". They were a husband and wife team who constantly argued and fought on the air and off. When- ever she would begin yelling at him, he would start to sing some aria to drown her out. The crew was tempted to wear ear-plugs when he began to sing. He sounded like a mouse being stepped on by a cow. The reason they stayed on the air for years was they, too, brought in their own sponsors.

Dave Yarnell was, and is, a creative and bright fellow. He decided it was time to goose up the programming at the station. One of the first things he did was to start the William F. Buckley show 'Firing Line'. I doubt that anyone else at the station had ever heard of Buckley before. Yarnell also created "MILLION DOLLAR MOVIE", which became a huge rating success utilizing RKO's large library of feature films. It was a brilliant merchandis- ing ploy. David and I tried different kinds of programs. Some worked, others didn't. We were determined to shake things up. We created a hip children's show called The Funny Company starring comedian Morty Gunty who had been a school teacher before he became a stand-up comic so the program became a combination of educational stuff, comedy sketches, films, and in- terviews. It was fun doing it and we both remained friends with Morty until his untimely death.

We also figured out that sports programming would not only get us new viewers but bring more money into WOR-TV. We produced the New York Giant football pre-season games for two years. No one had ever done that before anywhere. The Mara family who owns the Giants, were the fat cats in the market and barely tolerated these television nuisances. Their patronizing at- titude really got to us. They were uncooperative and made our jobs very difficult. Guess they didn't realize the importance tele- vision was to their franchise. Times sure have changed. It was interesting traveling to the various cities especially with the broadcasting team we put together. Chris Schenkel was our an- nouncer and we decided to audition former players and celebri- ties as our 'color man'. It was something that had never been done before. Finally Chris asked if I would meet and consider a former Giant player Pat Summerall as a potential 'color man'. Af- ter talking to Pat for five minutes I knew he would be great. It was his first broadcasting job but certainly not his last. Summerall be- came one of the greatest sports announcers and world famous. Whenever I would meet him in the street years later he never forgot to thank me for his start.

Doing the Giant pre-season games gave me the chance to meet the legendary coach of the Green Bay Packers, Vince Lom- bardi. Coach Lombardi (everyone called him that. No one dared call him Vince. I'm not even sure his wife was allowed.) He was an impressive, frightening man. Hell, if he scared his two-hun- dred- and ninety-pound players, you can imagine how a little New York Jew was to meet him. Chris, Pat and I stood at the fifty-yard line with Coach Lombardi before a game in Green Bay chatting away. We were speaking he was just staring. Suddenly, a flock of pigeons flew over and one of them let go and a pile of pigeon poop landed on my jacket. We all watched as it oozed down from my lapel. I was so embarrassed I felt like crawling into hole. Lom- bardi didn't say a word. He didn't have to. He just glared at me coldly, like I was a vile paramecium and he walked away without another word.

After our second frustrating year dealing with the Mara family, David received a phone call from Sonny Werblin. Sonny was co-owner of MCA, the world's largest talent agency. He was a mover and shaker. He had just bought the New York Jet football team and wanted to know if we'd telecast the Jet's pre-season games. He made a deal so attractive that we bailed out of the Giants and went with his new team. The Jets had just signed a new Quarterback named Joe Namath. Sonny was a showman and understood that pro-football was entertainment. He, also, laid out the red carpet for us and made WOR-TV feel welcome. The rest is history. Among the other sporting events we produced were 3 Muhammad Ali championship fights. Even though the boxing promoters at the old Madison Square Garden on 8th Avenue were sleazy types but the Champ was always good na- tured, bright and accessible. He had an amused gleam in his eye and a humor about his celebrity that was wonderful. He realized how important television was for him. We were going to telecast the Ali-Zora Foley fight. I mentioned to Muhammad, in passing, that I needed the fight to last at least seven rounds in order to get in all our commercials. He just winked at me and smiled. He knocked Foley out in the eighth round. What a guy.

Yarnell and I started the New York Mets baseball at Shea Stadium in 1962 which had just been built and WOR-TV won the rights to televise their games. "The Amazing Mets" were the worst team in baseball that year. Casey Stengel was their man- ager and half the time he slept in the dugout. He was no longer the great manager he'd been with the Yankees but was a great promoter and made the Mets a success anyway. While the sta- dium was being built no one asked us where we needed our cam- eras placed and our control room was underground so whenever it rained we were ankle deep in water. Opening day at Shea Sta- dium was unbelievable and sold out. It was raining and we heard that the bathrooms began to overflow. Sewerage was running down the aisles. The cameramen were standing on tip-toes. It was a mess but worked out in the end – no pun intended.

The most fun I had at WOR-TV sports wise was when I produced a wrestling series starring the fabulous Antonino Rocca. Rocca, at one time was one of the countries most popu- lar professional wrestler. When he put his famous Argentina Drop Kick on opponents it was all over. One day a very wealthy Greek husband and wife, who lived in Argentina and were Rocca's friends came to visit David and me. They offered to put up the money for a wrestling show to compete against the" World Fed- eration of Wrestling" which had a monopoly in the wrestling busi- ness.

41

They still do. The organization was run by Vince McMahon a crook and friend of Donald Trump's. Antonino decided to buck them and start his own wrestling franchise. Antonino believed, as did many other wrestlers, that McMahon was stealing money from his wrestlers and they were pissed at him. Years ago, wrestling was one of the most popular entertainments in early television (it still is). It was cheap to produce and gave the viewers and fans lots of laughs as well as the classic 'good guy versus bad guy' matches. Rocca was taking a big risk because the WFW made it clear that it would blackball any wrestler who tried to break their monopoly. Antonino was positive that they had screwed him out of lots of money and decided to take them on. As he was lining up a group of wrestlers David and I went to Sunnyside Gardens, an old arena in Queens, New York and rented it for our shows. We signed Lonnie Starr to be our announcer. Lonnie hadn't worked in years having been implicated in the record pay-off scandal while being a disc-jockey in NYC.

Lonnie was thrilled to get our offer and he and I made a great ringside team as announcers. It was without a doubt the funniest program we had on WOR-TV. Rocca put together a group of wrestlers who were angry at WFW or just didn't care. There was the usual 'Nazi' bad guy, the 600-pound Hobo in cov- eralls and other assorted psychopaths along with 'goody-guy' he- roes. Antonino Rocca was the star attraction. Frankly, I never had more fun in my life than I did doing this wrestling program. I would meet Antonino at this large apartment in NYC and we'd drive over to Sunnyside Gardens. He'd park his big Caddy in front and crowds of fans would surround him to get his auto- graph. We'd go inside and meet with Lonnie and go-over the matches and commercial break we needed. Lonnie was a very funny, likeable man who was quite fat and wore a terrible toupee. It was an easy prop for 'bad' wrestlers to pluck off his head during a match. I'd then go downstairs to the basement 'dressing room' and talk to the wrestlers and announce the time for each match. I had figured out what I needed to get all the matches and com- mercials in during the allotted time we had on the air. From the broadcasting table at ringside I would give the wrestlers a minute then 30-second warning. They had to end the match on time. No ifs, ands or buts. The wrestlers never missed a cue. They were amazingly disciplined. I never discussed who was going to win a match...that was their business. I would then go upstairs and sit down with Lonnie and we'd both light up big cigars and wait for the action. I've got to tell you that no feature film ever actually portrayed the dismal, filthy conditions of the dressing rooms and shower facilities in boxing and wrestling venues. The only way I would take a shower in one of those places was to be fully clothed in a hazard suit.

Anyway, the matches would begin and Lonnie would begin to make fun of the 'bad' guys. The audience at Sunnyside Gar- dens looked like escapees from padded rooms. They would scream, yell and throw things at the ring. A few of the really 'bad' wrestlers would object to the cigars Lonnie and I were smoking, so we'd blow smoke at them and they would jump out of the ring and chase both of us around the arena. I had the cameramen follow all this crazy action so the viewers at home could follow the crazy action and see us chased around. I loved every second of every match. It was show business at its finest. Sadly, after thirteen weeks our 'bankers' decided to pull out. It was obvious that a local broadcast of wrestling wasn't going to hurt the mon- olithic WFW. Too bad, because the evenings being chased by a Nazi will live in my memory. It was a joy.

It's safe to say that all remember where they were on Fri- day, November 22, 1963. When I heard of President Kennedy's death I was destroyed like everyone else. I, also, realized that David and I would have to stay on the air non-stop until his fu- neral. We contacted every constitutional scholar to discuss the history of murders of Presidents, how a new Vice President would be chosen once VP Johnson assumed the Presidency, etc. One of the people we contacted was Richard Nixon, who was the living in NYC. He came to the station with his own make- up man. I couldn't shake Nixon's hand. He repulsed me. Besides conducting interviews and putting together pieces of Kennedy's life, speeches and history. We stayed-up for forty-eight hours dealing with the 'live' John Kennedy. In fact we were editing tape (in these days video tape was 2 inches wide and when editing you used a razor blade to make an edit then scotched taped the two pieces of tape together. It was really primitive). Anyway, we had the news on when we were at work and watched Jack Ruby shoot Lee Harvey Oswald. In hind-sight it looked like the world was going crazy. Sunday night I was to go to a dinner party at Sally Barth's apartment. Sally and I had an 'on-again-off-again' love affair for almost ten years. We met in 1959 when I was still doing Pantomime Quiz and she was an editor at Vogue Maga- zine. Well, dead tired and exhausted from editing Kennedy's tape at WOR-TV I took a cab over to Sally's and slumped into a chair and had a drink. Needless to say, I wasn't very good company that evening. (More about Sally later in the book.)

The most prestigious thing we ever did at WOR-TV was to Produce the very first "TONY AWARDS SHOW" ever televised.

The Tony's are to theater what The Academy Awards is to Movies, the Emmy to Television, and the Grammys to the Music Industry. We did this TV special live from the New York Hilton hotel on a Sunday night. Every star on Broadway was part of the cast as well as the great names still alive in Theater history such as: Helen Hayes, Bob Fosse, George C. Scott, Lerner & Lowe, Richard Rodgers, Carol Channing just to name a few. It was a black-tie event and everyone was excited. I called an early rehearsal on Sunday morning so that all the presenters and nominees could walk through their paces getting used to entrances and ex- its. There's nothing worse than an Awards show where people stand around confused and don't know where to go. It also gave our cameramen a chance to rehearse their camera shots. Just to play it safe I decided to call another rehearsal in the afternoon. I didn't want any glitches. This was an important show. Richard Burton, who was playing "HAMLET" on Broadway at the time walked over to me and sheepishly asked me to do him a favor. One of the biggest stars in world was very professional and nice enough to ask me if I would allow him to miss the afternoon re- hearsal. He explained that he and Elizabeth Taylor had a poetry reading scheduled at the 92nd Street Y. but would cancel the poetry reading if I needed him. I assured him that I trusted him and that I would see him back at the Hilton before our show. The Tony Awards went off brilliantly and everyone was thrilled with the program. After the telecast they he came over to my table with Elizabeth and they both thanked me once again. She was gorgeous as she was in her movies. Burton said, "Arnold, you know the 'Jew-ass, don't you?"

My style as a producer was already forming. I was very organized, anticipating problems and most importantly putting to- gether a good staff to do the same. I have no tolerance for dilettantes and goof-offs. I always treated everyone as professionals and expected them to act like ones.

Our overall boss was a guy named Bob Leder. Bob was honcho at WOR-TV as well as head of RKO General Broadcast- ing a large broadcasting company. He was a helluva guy and we became close friends. He was also a power in the New York Re- publican Party. He once told me to get on a plane, fly to Wash- ington, D.C. and spend the day with New York Senator Ken Keat- ing. I tried to beg off because I had orchestra seats to "FUNNY GIRL", BUT Bob couldn't have cared less. My job that day was to observe Keating in action and recommend how Ken could im- prove his appearances on TV. He was going to have to improve, because Robert Kennedy had just announced as the Democratic candidate for Keating's seat. I was met at the airport by Keating's staff, taken to the Senator's office and followed him around all day. He turned out to be a very pleasant man. We had lunch in the Senate dining room and after spending hours with the guy had to tell him and his advisors the truth. I didn't think he had a chance against Bobby because Kennedy had the 'Kennedy myth' going for him and he was great on television. A casting director would have cast Keating in the role of a Senator in any movie. He had a full head of white hair, dimples and a nice smile but sadly was dull on camera. No personality came across.

There was no fire-sale on personality you either had one or not. Bob Leder, and the Republican party weren't happy with comments but they were accurate as Bobby Kennedy destroyed

Keating in the election. I never did get to see "FUNNY GIRL". The next trip Bob Leder had in mind for me turned out a lot better. Months later he announced that we were going to Palm Springs for a golfing vacation. I had never been to the California desert in my life and I looked forward to it. Getting paid and playing golf – not too shabby. The desert was absolutely gorgeous – breath- taking. There are mountains surrounded but lush greenery, cac- tus and sand. We checked into the Ocotillo Lodge, which was one of the 'hot' spots back then. We unpacked and rushed to the Canyon Country Club and teed off. When we finished and went back to the hotel we went to the pool, had a cocktail and looked up at the mountains. My heart stopped. The mountains were turning pink and purple. It was the most beautiful sight I'd ever seen. I vowed that one day I would live in Palm Springs. It took me ten years to get there, but it came true. I still live there now and still get goose bumps when I look at the mountains.

While I was still working at WOR-TV I got a call from West-inghouse Broadcasting. Guess my reputation as a good pro- ducer was getting around. They asked if I would screen a day- time talk show they were doing from Cleveland starring Mike Douglas. I looked at it and loved it. It was well done, the camera- work was great and Mike Douglas was a darn good host. Woody Frasier who had created the show was its producer but wanted to move on to other projects so they were looking for a replace- ment for Woody. They offered me the job and I accepted it. It meant I would have to move to Cleveland. Dave Yarnell, Bob Leder and the rest of WOR-TV wished me well. They also said that if things didn't work out I could always come back home. That was very comfort- ing and came in handy later on.

CHAPTER SEVEN

THE MIKE DOUGLAS SHOW

DID YOU EVER SPEND TIME IN CLEVELAND DURING THE mid-six- ties? If your answer is 'NO.' congratulations! The Black Hole of Calcutta would be considered a resort compared to Cleveland in these days. The Douglas show put me up in the Pick-Carter hotel which was dingy and depressing. So much so, that I flew back to New York each weekend to my apartment in London Terrace. Bob Leder used my apartment to entertain his girlfriends during the week. I was lonely every minute I was in Cleveland and the weather was dreadful. I realized from the start that I was not go- ing to be happy working on the Douglas show. It was a mistake taking the job. Douglas was a very nice, friendly guy. Everyone liked him. He had made reading cue cards into an art form. Al- most every question Mike asked guests were written for him on cue cards. Often he didn't have a clue who the guests were or why they were on the program.

It also became apparent to me that the Douglas staff worshipped Woody Frasier and weren't going to accept me as their new producer and boss. They were all nice enough but I was treated as an outsider and resisted any changes I wanted to make. Another problem was Woody was around all the time so that complicated my job. I gritted my teeth and tried to make my-self useful, but God I missed New York and my friends there. The only things I accomplished was when Dick Gregory was booked as a guest. Gregory, at the time, was the only Black comedian who was doing 'social satire'. He didn't pull any punches about what he saw with America when it came to its treatment of Blacks. While he was doing his hard-hitting monologue I had to go up to the production offices for a few things. Our phones were lit up like a Christmas tree. My mistake was who told him to fuck off and hung up. I figured what the hell and started answering more calls. They were basically racist rants about "nigger this and nigger that." After a while I didn't even listen to what they were complaining about. I'd just say, "Go fuck yourself!" It felt wonderful so I just remained in the office during the rest of the show telling viewers off. When the show ended and Woody and the staff dame back I was still at it. Obviously my days on the Mike Douglas show were numbered.

I called Westinghouse and told them that I wanted out of my deal. Since I had about 4-weeks left on my contract they asked me to fly to Los Angeles for them as a consultant on a new show they were just starting. Westinghouse had just replaced Steve Allen with a young, new talk show guy from San Diego name Regis

Philbin. They wanted to check Regis out and I would have flown to Moscow in order to get out of Cleveland.

Before I left, I suggested to Woody that he do something that I WILL BURN IN HELL FOR. The show's Associate Director was a bright, young kid who I thought was being wasted in his job and suggested that Woody name him Associate Producer of the Douglas series. The fellow's name was and is <u>ROGER AILES. HAD I KNOWN THAT ROGER WAS GOING TO TURN INTO A RIGHT-WING CONSERVATIVE PRICK WHO HEADED UP FOX NEWS – I would have ripped my tongue out of my face.</u> Just think if I hadn't opened my big mouth Roger Ailes might still be in Cleveland. <u>SORRY WORLD!!!!!</u>

CHAPTER EIGHT

REGIS AND OTHER PEOPLE

I WAS THRILLED TO BE IN LOS ANGELES. IT GAVE ME A chance to hang out with my two friends Sam Denoff and Bill Persky. I first met the boys when they worked at WNEW radio in New York. Actually, they were working with David Yarnell who was the pro- gram director at the radio station. Sam and Bill always wanted to be comedy writers and after moving out to the west coast they had already won Emmy Awards as writers/ producers of the Dick Van Dyke series by the time I came out for the Regis Philbin show. When I visited their set Van Dyke ran over to me and we hugged. I hadn't seen him in years. It became obvious to me that Los Angeles was the place I should be living. All of TV had moved out there.

My time on the Philbin show was an easy one. I was Westinghouse's 'consultant' which, meant I had nothing to do but 'consult'. The show wasn't very good. Regis was a doll, but even he would have agreed that he was in over his head. We got to like me and nicknamed me "Killer-Kane". Many, many years later I was the Supervising Producer on the daytime version of "LOVE AMERICAN STYLE" and ABC asked me to hire Regis on the show as an actor. His daytime series with Kathie Lee had just started and they needed some publicity. I was happy to do it. I hadn't seen Regis in over fifteen years but when he walked into rehearsal, he threw his arms around me and said, "Killer-Kane". What a memory.

I lived at the Sunset Marquis, a very Hollywood type hotel just off Sunset Blvd. It was frequented by actors getting divorces and New York types in for a movie. It was a small, very informal hangout and I had a blast there. Among the other tenants were: Van Heflin, Roy Scheider, Roman Polanski and Sharon Tate, and a few 'working girls'. Tiny Tim lived there whenever he came to L.A. for a TV gig. One evening he gathered us all around the lobby and entertained for an hour on his ukulele. He was a kick.

One of my suggestions for a segment on Regis's show was to show viewers a tour of 'famous star's' homes. Corny – but tourists paid a fortune each year to take those kinds of tours. I bought a copy of a map that they hawk on street corners all over Beverly Hills. I sent one of our pages out to arrange a location shoot. Later that day, I was in my office and the operator buzzed and said, "Cary Grant is on the phone for you." Yeah, right. I fig- ured it was a gag picked up the phone and a voice sounding ex- actly like Cary Grant asked, "Is this Mr. Kane?" I started to be a wise-ass with the person on the other end of the phone doing a bad impression of Grant, myself. The voice kept insisting that he was really Cary Grant and I finally dawned on me that he was. Holy shit! I was talking to the actual Cary Grant. It turned out that he had been at home when our page and location crew stopped by his house and asked them nicely to please not film his home because he relished his privacy and didn't want hordes of tourists swarming around. The crew suggested that he speak to me at the office since this was all my dumb idea. Mr. Grant was so nice that I quickly assured him that we wouldn't film his home. He thanked me and then asked if I could switch him over to the young page that he had talked to at his house. Cary Grant invited the kid to visit him at Universal Studios – he took him on a private tour and they had lunch together. Unbelievable. The kid didn't stop talking about it for the rest of the year. Who can blame him? Grant was a class act just like the movies he starred in.

The other incident that I will never forget was the segment the Regis show was doing on the latest fashions in women's underwear. The producers had invited a group of sexy starlets to model the undergarments. When the afternoon rehearsal ended they were send off to wardrobe to be fitted. I was standing with the show's director when we noticed that one of the girls – who was the 'Calendar Girl" for the Hollywood Palace TV show hadn't gone to wardrobe. She was startling beautiful with a body and skin to die for. We asked her why she was hanging around. She kept asking if she could meet Regis. We told her "NO." That Regis wasn't in the studio and for her to get into wardrobe. She finally left and her publicity man came over – I think his name was Pat... something. He begged us to let Regis interview her, even if it was for a few minutes during the segment. We ex- plained that if Regis interviewed her he'd have to interview each of the other girls and the segment didn't have the time. The guy wouldn't let up. He finally said, "Don't you realize how important it would be for her career?" We finally insisted that he bug off. I guess the guy was really desperate because he told us that if Regis did interview her, his client was prepared to sleep with him. We threw him out. What kind of show did he think we were run- ning? The young starlet, by the way, was Raquel Welch. I'm sure Miss Welch never knew what he said, but it really happened. It was the only time in my life that I wished I was Regis Philbin.

CHAPTER NINE

BACK IN THE BIG APPLE AGAIN

WHEN I RETURNED TO NEW YORK I DIDN'T KNOW what I was going to do. I didn't really want to return to WOR-TV. I'd been there, done that. So, I sat around waiting for something to happen. After a few months which seemed like years it occurred to me that the

U.S. Space Program was getting lots of news coverage. So far, no one had done a television series about the space program. The networks would cover a 'space shot' but that was the extent of it. I had the thought to do a series about our countries plans in space for the future. President Kennedy had pledged that America would land a man on the moon. It seemed like a commercial idea to me so I went to see my old pal Bob Leder at RKO General.

By then Bob has split from his wife and after meeting a French woman with beaucoup dollars which Leder liked a lot. She also insisted that "bald" was out and he immediately started wearing a toupee. It always amazed me that men who had been bald their whole life suddenly put a golf divot on their heads and no one was supposed to notice it. Anyway, Bob listened to my 'space' pitch and said he'd buy six SPECIALS for RKO. He then got on the phone with his friends at 7-Arts Productions, a Cana- dian television distributor and sold it to them. That morning I was unemployed and suddenly I owned six TV specials. I didn't know how to thank Bob and his new hair. He solved that problem when he announced that he was now my silent partner in the deal. We owned it fifty-fifty. The truth is I couldn't have cared less. I was back in show business. It just shows how crazy-making show biz is.

My euphoria was over when I realized I had a big, big prob-lem. I didn't know squat about the space program or how to get the project started. The only thing I knew about flight was having a few affairs with stewardesses.

My contacts at the Pentagon were nil and the same thing held for NASA. I needed to find someone who was wired with those funny people. I put out feelers and heard there was a for- mer Navy Blue Angel pilot now retired and running a cocktail lounge in New Jersey and who wanted to get into show business. I arranged to meet him at my apartment at London Terrace.

Enter E. Duke Vincent! Duke was the prototype of a Navy hotshot flier with a crew-cut, muscles and confidence galore. The thought of working with somebody named Duke tickled me – the only other 'Duke" I had ever met was a Doberman. Duke loved the idea of "MAN IN SPACE" - the name I had named the series.

He was certain he could contact the right people for us. I was bowled over by his energy and hired him as my writer. He'd come to my apartment every day – I had turned a closet into an office and he would sit there and write. While he was writing I would 'produce' which meant me saying to myself, "I hope I can pull this damn thing off." Duke made meetings for us at the Pentagon and NASA. I guess being a Blue Angel opens lots of doors. While Bob Leder was getting us office space, Duke and I flew to Washington and met with people we needed to know. Suddenly, the project had legs. We began planning location surveys and meeting men that we wanted to interview on our Specials. Through Duke's contacts we flew on military aircraft free of charge and lived in 'Officer's Quarters wherever we stopped. I hired Jerry Shaw to direct "Man in Space". Jerry later won a ton of EMMYs as director of Hollywood Squares. He was a wonderfully talented, funny, sarcastic and if crossed mean as a snake. What a team. A gay director, a writer who looked like a Mafia hit man, and a New York wise-guy producer.

We filmed everywhere. There wasn't a NASA or military facility we didn't visit. We interviewed every top scientist working on the U.S. Space Program and well as the astronauts. The amazing thing was that three relative strangers got along so well.

The only problem we ever had on our various trips was with an officious public relations director at Cape Canaveral. He got his nose out of joint because we were independents and not net- work hotshots. He tried to make things difficult but we just ig- nored the asshole. At the start of the Apollo manned missions no one had ever taken a camera up to the actual control module that was going to be home for the astronauts. That was until we got there.

We had to somehow get up to the top of the gantry where the space capsule sat on top of the rocket. Security was tight as hell.

Here's what we did: Jerry Shaw hid a small camera under his jacket and we approached the M.Ps. guarding the elevator which took you up to the module. They were heavily armed. Shaw and I began talking loudly about "Senator Vincent" from the Senate Space Committee and his intention of visiting the capsule and complaining what a sonuvabitch he was and that he never took "no" for an answer. Suddenly Duke made his entrance looking very important and in a hurry. Jerry and I welcomed the "Senator" and asked how his flight from Washington was? The M.Ps. looked very impressed. Without missing a beat "Senator Vincent" announced that he was going to look at the capsule and we were to accompany him. "I voted enough millions for this damn space project and I want to see it with my own damn eyes!" Before anyone could react, we entered the elevator, slammed the door shut and rose to the top of the gantry. We walked out and were in the 'Green-Room'. The rocket stood hundreds of feet in the air. I'm a little scared of heights so I wasn't too thrilled to be there. Jerry and Duke began filming as I held onto the rail for dear life. At any minute I expected to puke on the M.Ps. down below who would then shoot us dead. We got the film we needed, went down the elevator and left the area without anyone being the wiser. Oh, I forgot, "Senator Vincent" shook hands with the M.Ps" and told them they were doing a great job. Did we laugh when we got back to our motel. The incident proved again what industrial strength balls Duke had. He was a natural. I immedi- ately told him he was no longer just the writer – but I was making him co-producer of the series and my partner. Years later Duke Vincent became Aaron

Spelling's partner and a muti-mil-lionaire. He never forgets to tell people that if it wasn't for me he'd still be hustling drinks at his cocktail lounge in New Jersey.

While we were finishing editing "Man in Space", Duke mentioned he really wanted to write television comedy shows. I said, "No problem" and put in a call to Sam Denoff and Bill Persky who by then had created "THAT GIRL" starring Marlo Thomas and were just starting a new series "GOOD MORNING WORLD" about radio DJ's. The only thing memorable about that short-lived series is that it was Goldie Hawn's first acting job.

Sam and Bill had met Duke on one of our trips to the west coast for our space series. When I asked if they could help him with his comedy writing ambitions they invited him to come out to L.A. and write a 'spec' script for Good Morning World and that they'd teach him about the comedy writing business. Duke packed up his car and his wife and he headed to Los Angeles. The boys were true to their word and Duke became part of the new series. People did things like that in those days. They were generous with their help. Not so anymore. With Man in Space finished and on the air I began to get anxious about what I was going to do next. David Yarnell solved that problem. He had left WOR-TV and RKO General Broadcasting and had partnered up with Horn/Greiner two of New York's top fashion and commercial photographers and directors. Steve Horn and Norman Greiner wanted to break into directing for television and thought Yarnell could help. David sold a couple of TV specials to Clairol and asked me to produce and write them. For the next year we did one forgettable special and one very good one. The "GREAT MATING GAME" was about the singles craze sweeping the country. Advertisers were spending hundreds of millions of dol- lars a year trying to attract single men and women. Singles became a major source of income for many Fortune 500 compa- nies. Singles bars, restaurants, apartment building, cruises, etc., were becoming popular. Our Special told that story. We filmed in Manhattan and Beverly Hills. While we were on the Coast we filmed a segment at Steffinino's the hottest restaurant in Los An- geles. Nicky Blair a former actor was the host at the joint. He rolled out the red carpet for us. He closed the place one night and turned it over to us. He also invited every beautiful single woman in town and celebrity friends to be in our Special. The Show was featured in TV Guide and made me a very big man with Nicky Blair.

After David and I finished that Special I once again felt that I had to get out of NYC. The city was falling apart. In Feb 1968 my prayers were answered ... Sam Denoff and Bill Persky called from Hollywood and asked me to come out and work with them. They had just written a movie called "The Nose Job" and asked if I'd like to produce it? I was on the next plane to Hollywood.

CHAPTER TEN
CALIFORNIA HERE I COME

THE VERY FIRST THING I DID WHEN THE PLANE LANDED at LAX was to kiss the stewardess. She happened to be sitting on my lap at the time. That's an old joke but she wasn't. I felt so exciting to leave NYC and start a new career and life. I got a furnished apart- ment in the hills overlooking the city lights. I bought a red VW bug and grew a mustache. Unfortunately, the mustache made me look like a member of a mariachi band so it went pretty quickly but I did learn to play the trumpet.

As soon as I settled in, I called the friend I had given my rent-controlled apartment at London Terrace in NYC and told him to ship out some books, some clothes and my favorite painting. Everything else was his and anything he didn't want to donate to the Salvation Army. In my mind I had no plans of going back to Manhattan. It turned out I didn't return to the 'Big Apple' for over ten years. Los Angeles was everything that I hoped it would be. The weather was fabulous, the people friendly. It took a while to get used to going into a Supermarket fondle a zucchini and have strangers smile and say, "hello". In New York I was afraid to say a word to my neighbors...and they were relatives. The women were gorgeous and available. Persky and Denoff saved my life by bringing me out to Hollywood. I felt like a new man. Working with them at Desilu-Cahuenga Studios was unforgettable. The studio was home to almost every comedy series in television. Dick Van Dyke, Danny Thomas, That Girl, Mayberry RFD, Gomer Pyle, Hogan's Heroes, just to name a few. Desilu-Ca- heunga had a history of having feature films shot on the lot in- cluding "HIGH NOON". It had been turned into a TV studio which Lucy and Desi bought. The place was a real eye-opener for me. All the staffs were very friendly and if one of the series had a problem writers and producers from other series would help out.

It was almost like a family. Everyone ate at Hal's Studio Café which was the studio's ptomaine palace. The food was awful but the laughs we all had hanging around together made up for it. There was no caste system. You might find yourself sitting at a table with Danny Thomas or Andy Griffith. One day I was sitting with Sam and Bill chocking down a sandwich of 'mystery' meat when Danny Thomas sat down next to me. The boys introduced me and we sat around bullshitting when a very young, sexy extra walked by our table. Danny scoped her out, shook his head and said, "If I didn't want to fuck everyone in a skirt, I'd be named a Saint." "The patron Saint of condoms!"

Sam, Bill and I had several meetings with Columbia Pic- tures about The Nose Job. We talked budget, shooting schedule, etc. To make a long story short something happened and the movie was never done. I think they couldn't cast it. Hello? What was I gonna do now? I didn't want to and couldn't go back to NYC.

Sam and Bill told me not to worry as they were about to start writing and producing a TV Special starring Dick Van Dyke and bringing Mary Tyler Moore back to television. Mary's movie career had floundered and this was a chance for everyone to realize how talented she really was. It didn't matter that she had been brilliant as Dick's wife on The Dick Van Dyke Show. In Hollywood people forget easily and you become old news fast. The boys told me that I could write the new Special with them. Let me explain – through the years I had written some comedy material and I was funny, but had never written an actual script before. I considered myself a producer and a darn good one. But, me as a writer? The guys said, "relax" – we'll teach you. Like I said be- fore talented people in these days did generous things like that. They encourage new people. Before I knew it I was sitting at a typewriter and pecking away as the three of us the script for "DICK VAN DYKE & THE OTHER WOMAN". I'm embarrassed to say I wrote it with them – maybe I contributed a few lines, but most of the work was done by Persky and Denoff. However, the writing credit was very important, and allowed me to join the Writer's Guild. The Special was a smash hit and was responsible for Mary getting her famous series.

I liked everyone I met a Desilu-Cahuenga except for Marlo Thomas. Marlo was starring in and was the major owner of "THAT GIRL" which Persky and Denoff had created for her when she was an unknown actress. The reason they were asked to create a show for her was that, at the time, the recently passed Leonard Goldberg was head of programming for ABC. He was dating her. The series was a huge hit and young women all over the country tried to have "the Marlo look." But, the "Marlo" look was totally manufactured. In real life Marlo was very ordinary looking with a sallow complexion and it was obvious she had had lots of plastic surgery.

If you passed her on the street you would never recognize her. She would spend between one and two hours each day be- fore filming getting 'the face' put on by her make-up and hair peo- ple. I found Marlo to be a mean-spirited, abusive bully to many of the folks who worked on the program. She was the big boss and never let anyone forget it. What really turned me off was when she would humiliate my friends Sam and Bill. She would often yell at them in front of others and try to demean them at any opportunity. At cast readings if she didn't like a joke and they thought it was good, she'd say things like "what do you know about comedy?" This to the guys who created her show. She'd especially get into fights with Sam Denoff. Sam is a redhead and doesn't suffer fools lightly. After she made a bore of herself and was feeling guilty she would send Sam and Bill an expensive gift from Tiffany as if that like excused her rude behavior. Persky and Denoff could have opened a Tiffany discount store with all the 'forgive me' gifts she sent. It's a pattern that many bullies have. I told her off one day after she embarrassed them again. She was shocked and from that day on we rarely spoke. We would have another run-in a couple of years later on a TV Special that I pro- duced and wrote. It was delicious getting her to back down.

A personal note: Almost every night I would meet Duke Vincent at Steffininos's for a drink and to meet some sexy girls. In 1986 when I arrived there were still 'flower children' on Sunset

Blvd. Free sex was still in vogue and I took advantage of it. This, from a guy who when he lived in Brooklyn would blush when or- dering chicken breast. It was all fun and games and rarely did I ever see the same woman two nights in a row. Bill Persky once said, "a commitment to Arnie is buying a girl a second cup of coffee." That wild life style disappeared, like lox at a bris - when AIDS reared its ugly head. Nicky Blair still ran Steffinino's and I was still his hero after getting the joint in TV Guide. I may have been his hero but in all the years I knew Nicky and all the restau- rants he was involved in he never, ever bought me a drink. What can you expect from an actor?

In between writing variety specials for Sam and Bill I was offered my first job on a television series. They had introduced Duke and Bruce Johnson, who was Associate Producer on Good Morning World. Bill and Sam suggested that both of them might want to get together and try writing scripts. In the 60's and 70's shows didn't have huge writing staffs. On most series the bulk of the scripts were written by free-lance writers. They could make a good living writing scripts for different series. Not anymore. 99% of scripts today are written in-house by staff writers and produc- ers. Today, the free-lance outside writer is as rare as a good Hungarian meal. Anyway, Duke and Bruce wrote a few scripts and clicked as a writing team.

When "Good Morning World" was cancelled after one sea- son they weren't sure what they were going to do. Hello, Aaron Rubin! Aaron had created "GOMER PYLE" and was its producer. He wanted to spend other time on other projects of his and was looking for someone to take over for him. Persky, Denoff and Carl Reiner told Aaron to hire Duke and Bruce. Naturally, Aaron was nervous about them and their lack of experience. Gomer Pyle was a hit series. Carl, Bill and Sam 'guaranteed them'. If they couldn't cut it those three would take over the series and run it.

Like I said, in those days people were so damn generous and helpful to newcomers. Remember this: "the two most important things in becoming a success in show business is timing and luck!" Talent runs a poor third. Duke and Bruce were in the right place at the right time. Jim Nabors met and fell in love with them and the deal was set. Within one year of arriving in L.A. Duke was producing one of the hottest series on TV. The boys did wonderfully on the job and everybody was happy. At the end of the season CBS decided that Jim Nabors should have his own Variety series. The network was basically phasing out rural shows like Gomer and Green Acres.

Nabors was basically a singer who had lucked into acting. He had been a frequent guest on The Carol Burnett show and audiences and viewers loved him. CBS offered Nabors a tractor full of money if he'd do a variety show. He said he would but only if Duke and Bruce produced it. Not only did the guys know noth- ing about Variety shows but they had never stepped in a tape studio in their lives. CBS told Jim to forget it. Producing a variety show was an art in itself. The network wasn't going to entrust an expensive series to two unknowns. No way. Jim Nabors was the most loyal man I had ever met. He surrounded himself with peo- ple he liked and trusted. He told the network, "No Duke and Bruce – no show." CBS sticking to their guns immediately said, "We love Duke and Bruce" and they became the producers of the series. The regulars on the Jim Nabors Hour were Frank Sutton, Ronnie

Schell (who were on Gomer Pyle with Jim) and Karen Morrow a wonderful singer.

They also hired me for the writing staff. It was the only series I ever did that wasn't one of Sam and Bill's projects. The most important thing I contributed was to suggest that Jim make his entrance through the audience every show instead of from the wings. Everyone dug that idea and that's how each Nabors hour opened each week. Honestly, I was too interested in having fun and trying to bed each of the girl dancers on the series than concentrate on my writing job. I became obsessed with young, little girls who could bend their legs behind their head. It was stupid of me. At the end of thirteen shows it became apparent that I wasn't cutting it and we all agreed I should leave. It's not the only time my Libido got me into trouble. I am happy to report that Jim Nabors remained a friend until he passed away.

Fortunately, Persky and Denoff were about to start another TV special "THE FIRST NINE MONTHS ARE THE HARDEST" based on a comedy album they had written. The show dealt with pregnancy. I wrote it with them. It must be obvious by now that not only timing and luck are important in one's career but having a good "Rabbi" who looks out for you in vital. Rabbi Denoff and Persky were mine. The boys signed Dick Van Dyke to star in it. The cast was made up of real-life show business husbands and wives: Jimmy Farentino and Michele Lee, Ken Berry and Jackie Josephs and Sonny and Cher. It was their first acting job. I hate to tell you, but Sonny was a putz and Cher a dummy. They re- fused to hang out with the rest of the cast which was too bad. Based on their appearance on the special CBS gave them their own variety show.

I owed Bill and Sam everything. Can't imagine what would have happened to me without their support, help and love. Based on their generosity I always tried to give a helping hand to new writers when I began producing my own TV series. Whenever they would thank me, I would tell them to 'pass it on.' All of us are helped sometime when we are starting out and it's important never to forget that. It became an obsession with me when peo- ple I helped others. If they didn't and they started to believe their own publicity, egos and success and that hated to be reminded of their own humble starts. I'll talk more about those slime-balls later.

My career was going along nicely. My social life couldn't have been better. I made love in dressing rooms at CBS, NBC and ABC. Also, on many household appliances. Guess I was an equal oppor- tunity 'Shtupper."

CHAPTER ELEVEN

A WRITING PARTNER

WHEN GORDON FARR AND I DECIDED TO BECOME A writing team it was a new experience for both of us. I had known Gordon, hav- ing met him at producer Bernie Orenstein's house one Sunday. They were both from Toronto which seemed like a training ground for many talented writers and directors work- ing in Holly- wood at the time. Gordy and my experience, at that point, had been mainly in comedy/variety shows and specials. He's worked on The Hollywood Palace and had just returned from London where he had helped create the Tom Jones and The Petula Clark shows.

Writing with a partner is like getting married. You spend most of the day with that person and in order to get along you have to use tact, patience and lose all ego. You also have to learn to compromise a lot. A partnership is just that. It is two writ- ers trying to do the best job they can without hurting or demean- ing the other party. No matter what dumb thing they suggest – you pause and say, "Yeah, maybe that'll work, but let's keep try- ing." As the partnership continues you lose some of that 'walking on eggshell feeling' and are comfortable enough to yell, scream and disagree without making it personal. When it works it's a fab- ulous experience. You feed off each other. It's also less lonely than staring at a computer screen by yourself. When the partners have a fight, the guilty party usually sends some flowers or a box of candy. Not really, but you do kiss and make-up.

Bernie Brillstein became our manager. I had known Brill- stein for over twenty-years starting when he worked in the mail- room at William Morris' NYC office. Through the years Gordon and I had different agents, but Bernie remained our manager until the 90's. Until he died, Bernie became one of the most powerful men in the entertainment business. Sadly, he started to believe his press and publicity and we parted in an ugly way. I'll explain later.

Farr and Kane started getting jobs writing and producing summer replacement shows. It brought us in some really good money and we worked with a few talented performers. Among those shows were: "THE SUPER COMEDY BOWLS". These were two big budget Specials that aired the night of the Super Bowl. The ratings were incredible. It starred all of the big name pro football players along with a bunch of TV and movie stars. We had to tape the shows over several weeks because we couldn't get the players until Monday due to their playing sched- ules. It was a scheduling nightmare but great fun to do. We even talked John Wayne to appear on one of the Specials. Needless to say, it was exciting to work with "Duke" Wayne although he did spit on the stage a lot. He also made it very clear that he thought we had too many Black football guests on the show although he used the "N" word to express his displeasure. Anybody who was somebody wanted to appear on the Specials: Lucy, Jack Lem- mon, Walter Matthau, Bob Newhart, Carol Burnett, Danny Thomas, Dean Martin, Rowan & Martin, Goldie Hawn, Dick Van Dyke, Flip Wilson, Mary Tyler Moore - to name a few. The show business stars were more in awe of the athletes than the other way around. They all insisted on getting autographs and pictures with their favorite football player. On the first "COMEDY BOWL" Gordo and I wrote a sketch involving Joe Namath and Lucy. Lucy was a comedy genius and Joe was naturally frightened and nerv- ous about doing comedy but the thought of working with Lucy scared the crap out of him. The sketch involved Joe being brought into an emergency room after a terrible accident. Guess who play the emergency room nurse? When Lucy found out who her patient was all hell broke loose. She got so excited that she kept banging him on all his broken parts. It was broad and very funny. Lucy calmly told Namath to just relax and do what she told him to do. That woman forgot more about comedy than most people ever learn. She was incredible to work with.

"MAKE YOUR OWN KIND OF MUSIC."

One of the most creative and exciting series we ever did. It aired on NBC as a summer replacement show and starred The Carpenters, Al Hirt, The Doodletown Pipers and a young comedy team – Jay Tarses and Tom Patchett. We gave Tom and Jay their first job and had a lot to do with their later development as successful writer/producers. Sadly, the boys seemed uncomfortable when they became big hits knowing we had helped them early on. They were two of the slime-balls I mentioned earlier. Make Your Own Kind of Music was brilliantly produced and mounted. It looked so damn good on the TV screen.

We graphically used the alphabet to lead into musical numbers and comedy sketches. Gordon and I wrote all the scripts before production started. Just prior to our taping schedule he announced that he was taking his wife Lynne on a vacation to Europe. It was news to me but not wanting to have an argument I told him 'no problem' - I could handle to taping without him. I wasn't going to get any more money for supervising the tapings. What are friends for?

The tapings went very well until Karen Carpenter started acting up. She suddenly became a prima donna butting into areas that were no concern of hers. She'd ask, "Why are The Doodletown Pipers" wearing those costumes? "Why was Al Hirt do- ing a comedy spot?" Get the idea? One of my major faults has always been losing my temper and telling people off if I thought they deserved it. I was never political or played 'the game'. This tendency to let off steam hurt me later in my career. Anyways, I grabbed Karen's managers who were Executive Producers of the series and very good friends of mine and told them to call Karen off. That she was becoming a pain in the ass to everyone and that she should just learn her own lines and songs.

They hemmed and hawed and made excuses for her lousy attitude. I told them that the next time Karen caused a problem that I was walking off the show. Within five minutes she started bitching about the lighting on someone else's spot. I looked at the guys. They didn't say a word. I turned and walk out of the studio never to return. Despite the unhappy ending, Make Your Own Kind of Music was a groundbreaking series. Although Farr and I enjoyed doing these shows we wanted to soon branch out and write sitcoms.

"THE FUNNY COMPANY."

In 1971, Persky and Denoff asked us to join the staff on a new comedy series they had sold to NBC called "THE FUNNY COMPANY". It was a spin-off of a special I had written with them called "The Americans". The Funny Company was the best com- edy show of the season although no one watch it. It wasn't bad enough that we were against "Marcus Welby", one of the top rated shows on TV, we were also against a CBS sitcom named Funny Face which starred Sandy Duncan. Most viewers con- fused both "Funny Face" and "The Funny Company" as we were both cancelled. Marcus Welby must have laughed all the way to the bank. Mort Werner, then head of NBC said, "It was the best series I've ever cancelled." That didn't make us feel any better. Can you imagine a network boss admitting he was giving up on a great series? Dumb! Each episode had a subject that we ex- plored for the entire hour. For instance – The Funny Company looks at 'Love' or 'Money' or 'Marriage' or...you get the point. Gene Kelly was our host – a big name for television. We had four couples repre- senting different segments of the population as regulars. We had a senior citizen couple, a blue-collar couple, a yuppie couple, a black couple, and two teenagers.

Occasionally we would have a guest star like Jack Benny on the show. Besides the comedy sketches we had original mu- sic on every program. It might have been the best writing staff ever put together since the old Sid Caesar days. I got Jay Tarses and Tom Patchett jobs as junior writers on the Funny Company. It's too bad that the viewers never tuned in because they would have become fans. In order for a series to be successful you need a good time slot, if you don't you're off the air no matter the quality of the series. One of my fondest memories was when we had Jack Benny 'host' the show about "MONEY." The gimmick we came up with was that we had a real Brink's truck drive on stage and dump one millions actual dollars on the floor. It was real money! Jack just stared at it and stared. And finally a tear came to his eye. The audi- ence and we howled with laugher. Jack loved the bit and praised us for coming up with it. What a thrill.

CHAPTER TWELVE

THE SITCOM YEARS AND OTHER THINGS

GORDON AND MY FIRST SITCOM WAS FOR "THE NEW Dick Van Dyke Show". It was being shot in Cave Creek, Arizona. Dick had gone to live there on a ranch. Our old friends Bernie Orenstein and Saul Turtletaub were producing the series. Happily we found the new form of writing comfortable and easy. We also had the perk of being invited to Cave Creek when our script was in re- hearsal and taped to help with any re-writes. We stayed with Orenstein at his condo.

Why Cave Creek? Well, this small ranching community had this wonderful TV studio that the show could use and it was close to Dick's new ranch. He had tired of living in Los Angeles. None of the other cast members were thrilled at having to live in Arizona. Hope Lange, who played Dick's wife, in the series, was dating

Frank Sinatra at the time. Sinatra sent his private jet on Friday nights to bring her back to California. Hope was very pretty but one tough cookie who hadn't done a lot of comedies in her career. Dick started drinking very heavily by then, although known of us knew how much. Turns out he was boozing during the original series but Carl Reiner, Sam, Bill and Mary Tyler Moore didn't have a clue. Midway during the production schedule in Cave Creek Van Dyke awoke one morning and couldn't find his Jeep. He walked down his driveway and found his Jeep up- side down. He'd driven it back after rehearsal obviously loaded and crashed the Jeep. He climbed out, walked home and went to sleep. The next morning he realized what happened and real- ized that his drinking had gone too far. He could have been killed the night before. That's when he knew he was an alcoholic and announced it publicly. He was one of the first stars to admit to the illness. The series didn't get any ratings and was cancelled.

Gordon and I began to pick up other assignments. We were enjoying ourselves and beginning to make good money. We got a call from Brillstein, that Doug Cramer, who was the head of Television for Paramount TV wanted to see us. Oy Vey! Fasten your seat belts. I was the first of many projects we did with Cramer. Doug was very snobbish, wealthy, gay and a Gucci loafer wearing powerbroker. He was 'married' to Joyce Haber who was a powerful gossip-columnist for the L.A. Times. They were people you were warned never to cross or get on their wrong side. They could turn on you in a nanosecond. I speak from experience. Doug's repu- tation was as 'the velvet killer.' He never seemed to keep friend- ships for very long. Gordo and I were warned not to get too close because eventually he would try and destroy us. You would be 'one of his boys' until he no longer needed you and then look out. Our first meeting with Doug involved us writing a very important TV Special "A SALUTE TO OSCAR HAMMERSTEIN". It was to air on CBS on a Saturday Night. It was done in conjunction with The Friends of the USC Library." Every year, these wealthy people got together to honor someone special in the entertainment industry. Hammerstein had been dead for many years but was certainly a worthy sub- ject. It was a black-tie dinner held in the USC library building. It was very prestigious and I was thrilled that Doug asked us to write it. Gene Kelly as going to host the program, which was great since we had just come some off The Funny Company with Gene and he was comfortable with our writing.

Academy Award winning Director Robert Wise had agreed to direct the Special. While we were researching Oscar's brilliant composing career the show's booker lined up a "Who's Who" of show business to appear on the program. We decided that besides opening and closing monologues for Gene Kelly we would use all the guests as sub-hosts who would explain different periods of Oscar's brilliant composing career and life. Writing this show convinced me that Oscar Hammerstein was probably the best lyricist who ever lived. <u>Payback time!</u> A few days before we were to tape the Special I happen to be in Persky and Denoff's office schmoozing when Marlo Thomas called. They put her on the 'speaker phone' as she bitched about what we had written for her for the Ham- merstein Special. She asked them to re-write it. She obviously didn't know I was listening. Sam and Bill, holding on to their laughter asked her what was wrong with what we had sent her? That Gordon and I were great writers what the hell was her problem? She began to backtrack saying that she thought they could improve the material although it wasn't that bad...blah, blah, blah. I couldn't wait to confront her at the show.

Every guest star loved our writing. One of the wildest things happened that involved Robert Young before the Special. Young, of course, has been the star of Marcus Welby, for close to ten years and was one of the most famous actors around. I asked him if everything was okay with his stuff and he said he thought so. He then started counting how many lines we had writ- ten for him. All he cared about was that he had the 'same' number of lines as anyone else on the program. We could have writ- ten his stuff in Urdu and he wouldn't have given a shit as long as we didn't short him.

Enter Marlo Thomas. Her date that night was Henry Kissinger. Really. They deserved each other. When Marlo realized I was one of the writers she turned white. I asked her what prob- lems she had with her words. Would she feel better if we got some- one else to replace her? You have never seen anybody eat crow as quickly as she did. "No, I love the material. It's wonderful," Marlo answered. We did have a problem occur a few hours before we were to begin to tape the show. The stage hands union suddenly decided to pulls a strike. I guess they thought they could blackmail CBS for more money. I never did find out what caused the work stoppage. When Gene Kelly heard about the 'strike' he refused to cross the picket line and pulled out of the show. Doug Cramer, Bob Wise and everyone else panicked. Gordon and I told them to relax and quickly divided Gene's lines between a few other co-hosts and the Special went off without a hitch.

We had great ratings and reviews. Doug Cramer was thrilled that we pulled his pantyhose out of the fire. We saved the day. A short time later he left Paramount television for an inde- pendent production deal at Columbia Pictures and asked us to do a few projects for him.

The first job was a re-do of a pilot called "FRIDAY NIGHT GROUP" that had been shot the season before but didn't make the schedule. Doug and Columbia thought it had legs if we could fix it. After viewing the pilot Gordon and I could understand why the network didn't buy it. The cast was pretty poor and the writing just so-so. Gary Marshall had created it and wrote the pilot. He was a big time talent. He then became a huge success as a movie director until he passed away. But, in this case Gary's plate was full of other TV projects and he didn't have time to re- ally devote to a second pilot. "FRIDAY NIGHT GROUP" just wasn't one of his finer efforts. I had known Gary for years and we liked each other. Doug Cramer was looking to quickly get a series on the air and establish himself as an independent producer. He had brought this pilot with him when he left Paramount. Normally a failed pilot I not given a second chance, but with Doug's contacts and his being part of 'the old boys network', he pulled it off. The only person coming back was director Jerry Paris. Jerry had been the next-door neighbor on the original "Dick Van Dyke" se- ries and had developed into a very good and successful TV com- edy director. Gordo and I were hired to produce the new pilot and punch-up any scenes that needed it once Gary Marshall had turned in his script. We waited and waited for the re-write. We had re-cast the pilot and everyone was satisfied that we had a group of good actors. It was getting close shooting the pilot and Gary still hadn't turned in the script. I would call him and get some lame excuse. He was obviously stalling. Finally, I told him that unless we got the script in our hands that week Gordon and I would write the damn thing. At the end of the week his script arrived and it was lousy. Gary has a reputation of farming out scripts to writers in had on staff and maybe this was one of them. Cramer liked our version and Gary didn't seem to mind that we had 're-written' him. We began rehearsals and everyone seemed happy with the show.

We were Cramer and Columbia's fair-haired boys. We were told that Gary was going to attend the taping and 'warm-up' the audience with his comedy routine. It was something he did with all his series. I even played 'stooge' and his warm-up was a big hit. He seemed very pleased. The taping went very well and the audience response was fabulous. Doug and Joyce Haber took Gordy and me to dinner. Their compliments flowed like wine. After dinner we headed back to NBC to edit the pilot. Because of Gary's stalling we had to stay up all night in order to finish and get the pilot to the NBC executives in New York. Time was of the essence. Gordon and I worked all night and were bleary-eyed when Doug and Gary Marshall showed up the next morning to look at the finished pilot. Cramer has a few piddly notes but Gary began suggesting major changes. I was really tired and began to lose my temper at him. I told Gary that if he cared so damn much he should have stayed up with us all night when we edited the show. I didn't appreciate him coming in after the fact and suddenly being so concerned. I also reminded him about his stalling getting us his lousy script which we had to totally re-write. I told you I had a bad temper. Marshall was stunned. I guess he wasn't accustomed to someone speaking to him like that. Obviously I was over-reacting and it wasn't a very smart thing for me to do. I was always a problem for me to keep my emotions in check. Gary Marshall never forgot my diatribe and he would never work with me again. Oh, by the way, the pilot didn't sell.

Gordon and I created a pilot called "KEEPING UP WITH THE JONESES" and we partnered up with Doug Cramer and Columbia. It was about two families who shared a brownstone. One of the families was a black couple played by John Amos and Theresa Graves and the second was a white blue-collar couple played by Warren Berlinger and Pat Finley. It was one of the first multi-racial series ever tried. We had worked with these actors on the Funny Side and like their work a lot. Jerry Paris once again directed it for us. We couldn't have asked for anything better. When we turned in the Pilot to the Network they really dug it. Columbia, Cramer and we were confident that we had a winner. "KEEPING UP WITH THE JONESES" was on the early fall schedule. Less than 5% of the pilots shot every year every make it on the air. We were flying high. We shouldn't have counted our chickens before they were plucked.

Columbia was given a choice by NBC. They could have our half hour on the schedule or an hour pilot they had done called Ghost Stories with William Castle as the host and creator. Castle was a long-time director of horror motion pictures. Columbia, in their wisdom took the one hour offer and our pilot was passed on. Gordon and I were devastated. All our hopes and dreams dashed. Ghost Stories didn't work and was soon cancelled. There's no telling how my career would have worked out if "KEEPING UP WITH THE JONESES" went on the air. I felt like Marlon Brando did while playing Terry Molloy in On the Water- front. "I coulda been a contender." Easy come, easy go.

By this time Doug Cramer had sold a series called "BRIDGET LOVES BERNIE" to CBS. It was a rip-off of the old theatrical chestnut "Abie's Irish Rose." A Jewish boy marries a Catholic girl and the trials and tribulations of their new marriage. Bernie Slade, a friend and another Canadian, wrote the pilot but smartly declined to get involved with the series. He was happy collecting his handsome royalty. Bernie loved to sleep late. He made a great career out of writing pilots but never working on the series. He went on to write a few Broadway hits including Same Time Next Year. Slade died last year in Canada. "Bridget Loves Ber- nie" was given a great time slot and became a huge rating hit even though no one in the business liked it. Cramer asked us to take it over and fix whatever was wrong with it. It bothered Doug that 'insiders' hated the show. It was our first network series to actually run. David Bernie who played Bernie was not a happy camper and continually put down television. Meredith Baxter played Bridget. She was a nice actress and easy to work with. Her wealthy Catholic parents were played brilliantly by David Doyle and Audra Lindley. The Jewish in-laws were not only badly cast but there were too many of them. All in all the scripts had to service eight actors all of whom thought they were the stars of the show. Gordon and I decided to change the direction of the series. We started to write scripts that dealt with the newly-weds. They were the money to us. To hell with all the Jewish in-laws. Bridget Loves Bernie ended its first season as a top ten show and was guaranteed a pick-up.

We informed Cramer and Columbia that we'd only come back if we could 'ship' Bernie's family to Florida and bring them back if a story required them. We didn't feel we could do this hit series unless they allowed us to make changes. We had meet- ings with

CBS in Los Angeles and told them how we felt and why. Columbia and Doug were in our corner. The CBS execs yelled and screamed, "How the fuck can we tell Freddie Silverman that you want to change the series?" (Yes, the same Mr. Silverman. He kept reappearing in my career like a cold sore.) We explained to CBS that they could get new Producers but in good con- science we didn't think the show worked as constituted. Word of our ultimatum went around the business and we kept getting calls congratulating us. The decision was taken out of Silverman's hands. In one of the most bizarre things ever to happen in TV William Paley who owned CBS was tired of getting out of his limo each day and having to walk through a picket line of angry Ha- sidic Jews on the way into his building. These characters were protesting that any Jewish boy had married a gentile girl. They didn't want CBS to broadcast the series. Paley, who was Jewish, but didn't like admitting it decided to take things into his own hands. He announced he was going to screen every episode at his home in Jamaica and decide the program's fate. He had the tapes shipped to him, screened them and cancelled the series.

He didn't want to be embarrassed anymore. His society friends might not invite him to their next party. It was the only time a top ten series was thrown off the air.

I don't want to leave the impression that my life was all work and no play. I was dating some of the most attractive women in Hollywood. Many were starring in their own TV series or motion pictures. I was like a kid in a candy store. It was during that period that I rented my first house in the Hollywood Hills. No more apart- ments for me. It was a lovely bachelor house. It was very airy with an unbelievable garden and pool overlooking the city.

My next-door neighbor was Vincent Price. Vincent was a terrific character actor and a gourmet chef. I also began to spend most weekends in Palm Springs or at Bernie Brillstein's pool. Bernie and his wife Laura, who ran his office were great hosts. Their home and pool were jammed with clients, friends and family. It was great fun.

David Yarnell had moved to Los Angeles from NYC so the old gang was together again. Persky, Denoff, Yarnell and me. David asked me to meet with a young guy who had come out to direct a New York Met/Los Angeles Dodger game. David knew Chick Mitchell from WOR-TV. Chick and his partner Geoff Neigher wanted to become television writers. I was happy to meet Chick and see if I could help. We immediately connected and became fast friends. I suggested that when Mitchell got back to NYC that he and Geoff try to write a 'spec' script for the Mary Tyler Moore series. I gave them so copies of my own scripts so that they could learn the form and told him that once they finished their 'spec' script to send it to me. They did and I called them with suggested fixes. They made those fixes and sent me the new draft. I knew many of the producers at MTM Productions (Mary's production company) and sent Chick and Geoff's script over to them with my recommendation. MTM liked their work and hired them to write scripts. Chick and Geoff always considered me their 'writing father'. I was proud of them and later success as writer/producers.

Brillstein and Laura Brillstein decided to get Gordon and me the job as producers of a new NBC series starring Diana Rigg. Diana had become a star after playing Mrs. Peel on "The Avengers". She had been a star in the London Theater for years. The Brillstein's actually forced ICM, our agents at the time to hire us for the show. They refused to leave the office if ICM's head of television until the deal was done.

A very strange but talented man had created the Diana Rigg series ad was its Executive Producer. Leonard Stern was a very successful packager of comedy shows. His most famous was "Get Smart". In our new series Rigg played a British woman fleeing an unhappy affair in England and wound up living in her millionaire brother's penthouse apartment in NYC. Diana's char- acter gets a job as a designer in a 5th Avenue department store. Not the most exciting idea for a new television series but 'what- thehey'. The series dealt with her life in a strange city with a new job. At the time, Leonard had three other series on the air so he was spread pretty thin. He was a terrific writer although he could become infatuated with his own brilliance. Gordon and I were overjoyed to get the job and having the opportunity of working with Diana. She was very tall, very sexy and a great dame. Stern had put together an excellent cast of Broadway actors to support Diana. Everything was fine except that the time slot NBC stuck us with made all of us know we were going to have an uphill fight to make the series a hit.

I fell madly in lust with Diana and we became good bud- dies. She had just gotten married for the first time to an Israeli painter. He was a typical "Sabra" – opinionated, angry and stub- born. Not a nice fellow. I tried to get into Diana's knickers and she laughingly told me to at least wait until the honeymoon was over. Diana was a lusty woman with a vocabulary that would make a boatload of Greek sailors blush. She was marvelous fun to be with. During the series she and I would go out to dinner a lot and I invited both of them over to my house for parties. At one of them, 'Menachem' really began to act like a bore and jerk and I asked him to leave.

He huffed-and-puffed but finally got his coat and looked at Diana expecting her to leave with him. She told him that he'd been a swine and she had no intention of leaving a fun party because of his rude behavior. (My kind of woman.) We began production with Robert Moore, as not only one of the ac- tors in the series but the show's director. Moore had won a Tony Award for directing "BOYS IN THE BAND" on Broadway. Bob Moore was openly gay and hysterically funny besides being a great director. One of the problems the series had besides a lousy time slot was that Leonard had placed Diana on a pedestal in real life and wouldn't let us do stories about her dating men or getting involved in situations that a normal single woman might find herself in.

She finally complained to me that it was getting ridiculous. Why wasn't she getting involved with men, "Darling, he has me acting like an untouchable virgin. Trust me I am not." I told her to talk to Stern. She did and finally we were given the green light to make her a real person. Doing the series was a joy. The cast was great. However, the reviews of the series were awful. The news- papers didn't think a sitcom was befitting someone with Dian Rigg's talents. They were entitled to their opinions, forget- ting that Diana was a working actor who wanted to try comedy. Things got worse when the ratings came out and the series was third in its time slot. Another problem was that NBC was the lowest rated network at the time. Leonard quickly saw the writing on the wall and suddenly wasn't around that much. He began to distance himself from the show although he still insisted on doing the final re-write of each script. He would put in "Leonardisms" which were cutesy puns and word games. It was easy to tell his work from ours. Gordy and I were also required to take first edits of the show to NBC and screen it for Larry White who was head of television at the time. Larry was a buddy of Stern's and had bought his other three series. Larry would sit through the screenings and complain, "Leonard is up to his cutesy shit again." Farr and I had no experience with Larry White before so we became his whipping boys. Leonard was covering his ass and allowing us to take the heat. It was obvious to anyone who knew the scene that Farr and Kane were going to get the blame for the series that was failing. The Diana Rigg show was cancelled after 13 shows. I have nothing but fond memories a fine cast and a great leading lady.

While we were doing the Rigg series Bernie Brillstein set up a lunch appointment for us with Irv Wilson. Irv was one of the partners running a syndication company called Viacom. Viacom has since grown unbelievably big and now owns Paramount and CBS. Irv was looking for a comedy anthology series like "LOVE AMERICAN STYLE" which had finally ended production. Gordy and I went back to our office and kicked around several ideas and finally created a presentation for a series we called "THE LOVE BOAT". (Hold on to your cummerbunds, friends) Our cruise ship had regulars such as a Captain, a doctor, a social director, first mate, etc. It seemed like a funny idea to us. We met with Brillstein and Irv Wilson told them about our idea and showed them the presentation we had created. They flipped and Irv immediately went out to sell it.

Unfortunately, he found out it was too soon after Love American Style for the same type of series to get on the air. The idea reverted back to us. We figured we'd wait awhile and then try to sell it ourselves. While we were waiting for Bernie to get us another producing job, I bought my first home in the Hollywood

Hills. It was very formal and traditional with 3 bedrooms, an office and a glorious pool on the second floor. It was quite a place for a kid from Brooklyn. Two of my neighbors were Richard Pryor and Michael Eisner (former boss at Disney.)

We kept trying to create new series ideas and went to visit our old friend Doug Cramer who had moved over to 20th Century Fox. We told Doug and his young 'assistant' Bud Baumes (Doug always seemed to have young gay assistants.) about "THE LOVE BOAT", but Doug passed. He didn't think he could get a deal so soon after "Love American Style" which he had sold when he headed up Paramount Television. Gordo and I decided to try to give it a shot anyway. We set up a meeting with Andy Segal. Who was head of ABC comedy development. We pitched it to Andy, who laughed a lot but agreed that it was too early for that kind of anthology to be put into development. We thanked him and realized that "THE LOVE BOAT" would have to wait for a few seasons.

Anxious to get something going I called John J. McMahon who was in charge of NBC on the west coast. John was a good guy and an occasional drinking buddy. When I got him on the phone he told me the worst news I had ever received. John in- formed me that Larry White had told him that Gordon and I were no longer welcome at NBC. He blamed us for the failure of the Diana Rigg Series. Obviously Leonard Stern had done a lot of damage to our reputations. Gord and I were knocked for a loop. How could this happen? Each season there are many shows that don't make it but you don't get blackballed because of them. It's amazing how fast bad news spreads quickly in Hollywood. Sud- denly, Farr and Kane were untouchables as far as all three net- works were concerned. We couldn't get any job. I didn't know what to do. My whole life was wrapped up in work. Work was my validation. I couldn't tell anyone about how depressed I was – it would show weakness.

In the midst of this horror, Bernie Brillstein arrived at my front door with a suitcase. His wife Laura had left him for her gynecologist (fill in your own joke). In a wink of the eye my manager moved in with me. He was a basket case which made two of us. He would lie in bed all day eating and smoking. He stopped going to his office. And as much as I sympathized with him I also got pissed off because he wasn't working to get me a job! If I had a brain I should have thrown him out on his head! To top it off, Gordon called and said that Lynne Farr had gone to see the pro- ducer of The Bob Newhart Show seeking a writing assignment. He told her he'd give her one, but only if Gordon wrote it with her. Farr asked me what he should do. I told him to take the fucking assignment – that right now we were lepers and he might as well grab the loot. He wrote the script with his wife...it turned out really well and they were offered the job as story editors of Newhart. That meant our partnership was over although we swore we'd work together again soon. I now not only couldn't get arrested but had lost a partner. I had to start all again but as a single writer. Brillstein finally pulled himself together and started working again. It was obvious that I had to sell my house. I couldn't afford the mortgage payments and that maybe a change of scenery would be helpful. Fortunately the house sold quickly and I rented a wonderful apartment in an art deco building in Hollywood. With all the shit I had gone through I somehow felt strangely optimistic. It's amazing how people in show business are able to keep re- bounding from adversity. We almost become used to it. Some smart dude once said, "It ain't a business for the faint of heart." Amen! I felt like a new man: A new apartment...I bought myself a new car. (I always believed a person should give themselves a present when they feel down. A new car was better than a new pair of shoe laces).

I didn't have to wait long – Sam Denoff and Bill Persky called and said that they had just sold two new series - one to CBS the other to NBC and would I like to do one of them? Duh! I chose the one on NBC called "SUNDAY NIGHT DINNER". It was the story of a very emotional Italian family that got together every Sunday night for dinner. Writing for ethnic families is al- ways great fun because they are passionate people. Larry White had been fired from the network so I was allowed back to work there. His replace- ment Marvin Antonowsky was the prototype of a "nerd". He turned out to be even worse than Larry White. His creativity was on a par with a pot of kasha. Susan Harris, a great writer and creator of TV shows like "Golden Girls" called Marvin "The mad programmer" on the Johnny Carson Show because Marvin had just yanked the plug on one of her series. Anto- nowsky was fired after one year on the job. He visited us at our production office and announced that Sam and Bill's series was no longer called "Sunday Night Dinner". When they asked him why, he said that the title didn't test well. It turned out he was a statistical and testing expert but had no expe- rience with creative people. "Did you explain what the series was about when you tested the title?" Marvin shook his head, "No." He then went on to tell everyone the series was now called, "THE MONTEFUS- COS." Wow. What a catchy title but what does it have the fuck about an Italian family having dinner on Sunday Night? Sam and Bill's sarcasm went over his head and we wouldn't discuss the title change any further. He was NBC and they were only the creators. Is there any surprise the schmuck was fired so quickly? "The Montesfuscos" was a wonderful series to do. We all had lots of fun writing it and the cast were great. Unfortunately it was opposite the top rated show in the country and sank to the lowest rating of the year. It got so bad that Johnny Carson used the series as a butt of nightly jokes. Antonowsky didn't even have the class to cancel the "Montefuscos" correctly – if there is such a thing. He called and said pull, the plug immediately. We explained that we were in the middle of rehearsal and that we would NBC's decision at the end of the day. Marvin said, "No way." Unless we stopped everything right then NBC wouldn't pay for the rehearsal time. We all walked down to the studio and told the cast the news that it was over! One of our production assistants happen to take a picture as the cast learned the news showing the shock and horror on their faces. It shows what a brutal busi- ness is it is. The "Montefuscos" enabled me to buy a condo in Palm Springs. I've had a place in the desert ever since.

The old cliché "What goes around comes around" is deliciously true. I got a call from my agent (I don't remember which one except he was probably short). I couldn't have been more surprised if I found a nose in my soufflé. Larry White (you remember that boy chick) wanted me to re-write a pilot that Jimmy Breslin had written for him called "No Heavy Lifting." This is the same Larry White who was responsible for me being unwelcome at NBC and for being out of work for quite a while. He now wanted me to write something for him. Is it any wonder that folks working in TV are crazy nutcases? He sent over the Breslin script which wasn't really a television script at all but more like one of his great columns. Jimmy Breslin, until he died, was one of the finest writers and columnists in the country but he knew about as much as writing television scripts as I did about the history of spats. The Breslin pages read like a novel. It was very funny with wonderful characters but couldn't be produced as is. I had a fan at CBS named Alan Wagner who insisted that Larry get me to re-write it. Alan was always a wonderfully kind and generous man who be- came a friend and remained so until his death. I informed my agent to inform White that I would do the re-write but I wanted more money than anybody had ever gotten for a re-write. I also wanted to meet with him and discuss our past problems. White and I met in his office at Columbia and he couldn't have been more charming. When I asked him why he did what he done to Gordon and me Larry claimed ignorance. He didn't know what I was talking about. He never would have barred anyone from his network.

The man was either a great liar or had Alzheimer's before it was even discovered. I re-wrote the pilot keeping Breslin's fla- vor – but re-wrote it totally. White and CBS were thrilled. Alan Wagner sent me a letter of thanks. Suddenly, it occurred to me to ask if anyone had informed Mr. Breslin that his work was being re-written by another writer. Jimmy was a not only a famous writer but successful novelist. He might be a tad annoyed with what they had done. When they finally told Breslin he went crazy. He not only threatened to sue everyone's asses off he went on Johnny Carson and blasted CBS. That was the end of the pro- ject. I had gotten lots of money from Larry White although he never apologized for what he done to me and Gordon. The "NO HEAVY LIFTING" script I had written was pretty damn good and would have made a helluva series.

After the Montefusco experience Bill Persky decided that he wanted to concentrate on becoming at television director which meant that he and Sam Denoff split as partners. I know Sam was pretty shocked by Bill's decision They had been to- gether for over twenty years. Sam and I decided to write a Pilot for ABC together called "IT'S ME KIMMELMAN". It never sold because we couldn't cast it. Working with Sam was a total kick. We had been friends for years and enjoyed each other's company and humor. More to come.

PICTURES
OF
CELEBRITIES

CHAPTER THIRTEEN

ALICE AND A FEW OTHER THINGS

IN THE SPRING OF 1976, I BUMPED INTO BRUCE JOHNSON who had split from his partnership with Duke Vincent. (I told you writ- ing partnerships were like Hollywood marriages. Don't unpack.) Bruce was doing the pilot ALICE for Warner Brothers. It was based on the successful motion picture "Alice Doesn't Live Here Anymore". He told me that if the pilot sold to CBS he wanted to do the series with me. ALICE sold. The series starred Linda Lavin and had a great cast: Polly Holiday was Flo, Beth Howland as Vera, Vic Tayback as Mel and Philip McKeon as Alice's son. Beth and Vic had been in the motion picture. Unlike the huge writing staffs on today's shows we just hired one staff writer. The other scripts were farmed out to independent writers. Everyone was excited about the series. Alice had a fantastic Sunday time slot and CBS had predicted the series would be a huge hit. A good time slot will do that for you.

One day Bruce and I were having lunch at the Warner's café when Carl Reiner stopped by our table to say hello. Carl was directing 'OH, GOD" at the studio starring John Denver and George Burns. When he found out what we were doing and with whom Carl wished us a lot of, luck and said we'd need it. It turned out he'd directed a play on Broadway with Linda Lavin and found her totally unpredictable. According to him, she would never say the same lines two nights in a row. She had a nasty habit of ad-libbing and throwing her fellow actors. I want to be clear—Carl Reiner said those things not me. Reiner never knocked people and what he said shocked us. Bruce and I prayed she wouldn't pull that on Alice. (Turns out we didn't pray hard enough.) Warner Brothers Television was a nice place to work. It was run by Tom Kuhn and he had a staff of bright executives among who was Kim LeMasters. Who became a great friend and one day head of CBS Television. Alice was the first tape show to originate from a film lot. Bruce, Linda and I flew to Phoenix where the series was set. We looked over locations for our opening titles. The three of us got along very well so we began to discount Carl Reiner's warning. Big mistake!

When we got back Bruce and I began to give out writing assignments and started a few in-house scripts. I wrote biographies of our all our cast. It's something I find helpful for the actors as well as the writers we were hiring. When I handed them to our cast – Polly Holiday handed me one she had written for Flo. Amazingly, ours were almost identical. A great sign that, we were on the same page about her character. She was the only actress I ever met who did that. I knew she would be fabulous in the part of Flo and she was. Vic Tayback loved my insights about Mel and did everything that was ever asked of him. Beth Howland did the same thing with her part. Linda Lavin read hers and never mentioned it.

Bruce hired Carlinda Agrella as our production secretary. Carly had worked for him on the Jim Nabors Hour. Through Carly I met Hallie Stich who was working as head of publicity for Warner Brothers TV. We started to see each other and continued to do so for years on and off. She eventually became the first and only ex-Mrs. Kane in 1994. We began production and everything seemed okay. The scripts were funny and the actors were doing a fine job. Polly became an instant star playing Flo. Beth was cute as hell as the nervous Vera and Vic Taybeck was wonderful as the boss, Mel. He had kicked around for years as a character actor and suddenly was on a hit series and loved every second of it. God bless the time slot. CBS, however, was not as happy as they should have been. Something about the series wasn't jelling. The scripts read funnier than the shows played on the air. The problem turned out to be the unnamed actress playing the lead. (See I didn't forget my lawyer's warning.) She was going through a messy divorce and perhaps the pressure of that and starring in her own series got too much for her. It doesn't give me any pleasure to talk about Linda this way. Personally she was a nice woman but began to reverting to her habit of adlibbing and doing whatever came into her head during a show. (Carl Reiner predicted this.) When asked why she was doing it she would just shrug and say that she just felt like it. The other actors were get- ting annoyed with this especially Polly Holiday. It was unfair to the other actors because they never knew what was going to ex- pect from Linda. Bruce and I had several meetings with CBS to discuss the problem and explain that she was becoming a loose cannon. Steve Mills, the CBS executive in charge of the show didn't believe us and was convince that we need help on the se- ries although he didn't mention it.

The show was getting big ratings but everyone though it should be better. One morning Bill D'Angelo, Ray Allen and his partner Harvey Bullock walked into our offices as the "new Executive Producers" of Alice. Bruce and I were obviously surprised but knew there wasn't much we could do about it. It turned out to be a blessing in disguise. Not only was Bill D'Angelo a brilliant producer but Ray and Harvey were great writers. They helped the show immensely. Bruce must have seen the handwriting on the wall and decided to leave Alice soon after the boys arrived. He had gotten a wonderful offer from Gary Marshall to come over to Paramount to work on his shows. It was a smart move on Bruce's part as he stayed at Paramount for over twenty years. One Gary's series that he produced was "Mork & Mindy". Bill D'Angelo took over the ugly task of trying to keep Linda Lavin in check as well as running the production. I nicknamed Bill "Nero" because the loved having an entourage following him around. We became best friends until he passed. Ray Allen and I fell in love with each other. He was cranky, funny and sarcastic and had a heart as big as Yankee Stadium. We discovered we were kindred spirits. Harvey Bullock was a nice, sweet man who didn't mind when Ray and I decided to do the re-writes together. Ray and I would sit around with tears pouring out of our eyes laughing so much. The problems with our star continued and that was Bill's responsibility.

One of the funniest moments on the series came when I flew my parents out to visit. I had written a two-parter about Alice being visited by her pain-in-the-ass former mother-in-law. By then Warner's had replaced Tom Kuhn with a former casting director named Alan Shayne. Shayne was a treacherous man to work for. He was very sneaky. He insisted on casting Eileen Heckart as the mother in law. I had written a Jewish Betty Kane type. Eileen was badly miscast and not very pleasant to work with. My parents came to the show and the cast knew where they were sitting and during the taping, they kept peeking out to see what my Mother's reaction might be. During one of the scenes Heckart said to Alice, "You never liked me." "That's not true." "Yes it is. Remember when you sent my husband a Father's Day card?" "Yeah, and I sent you a Mother's Day card, also." "But his cost more!" "What?" "His card cost more money. I looked at the back of the card and saw that was true." Alice just rolled her eyes in the show and the audience screamed with laughter. I looked at Bea Kane and there was no reaction. My Father, Murray, tried to hide his laughter. At the end of the taping I asked them how they liked the show. They complimented it...but my Mother said she though Eileen was too unbelievable. Unbelievable? My mother had actually said that about to card to me.

D'Angelo had taken over as Director of the series trying to keep a lid on Lavin's ad-libbing and behavior. The rest of us were in The Green Room during a rehearsal, when John Rich walked in. John was a famous Director and had won lots of Emmy awards. John informed Ray, Harvey and me that Alan Shayne had asked him to observe the show and recommend how to fix it. This was news to all of us. Shayne has sent Rich all our scripts without our knowledge hoping that John Rich would say they weren't any good and were what was wrong with the series. John was known for not bullshitting. If he hated something, you'd hear about it from him. We taped the first show and it went reasonably well. After a dinner break, we taped the second show. Suddenly, in the middle of one scene Linda began to cry. The problem was it was a comedy scene and she hadn't cried during the first taping. She 'decided' to try something else during the second show. Rich couldn't believe his eyes. We explained that she did that a lot and refused to do two performances the same way. John Rich left shaking his head. He had never seen anything like that in his long career. The next morning; Alan Shayne. Linda and John Rich had breakfast in Malibu. They thought that John would say the scripts sucked and that was what was wrong with the series. Instead John Rich told Linda Lavin that she was the most unpro- fessional actor he's ever seen. That there was only one problem with the series and he was looking at her. The scripts were ex- cellent and Warner's was lucky to have us writing them. John later told me that Lavin began crying. I don't think that's what Shayne or Lavin wanted to hear. Like I said John doesn't pull his punches. For going to one taping and reading a few scripts John Rich got a very healthy royalty on every episode for the rest of Alice's ten-year run.

We were really powerless to discipline Linda. She had Alan Shayne in her corner. It was a struggle to get through the rest of the season. I had decided not to come back the following year because the job had become a drag. During the last week of taping Polly Holiday called me and asked me to come down to the stage. When I arrived I could tell Polly was furious. For some reason D'Angelo, Ray and Harvey were out of the office. The actors ran through the scene they were rehearsing. Suddenly, Linda began doing a Southern accent imitating Flo. I asked why she was doing it? It didn't call for that in the script. Lavin said she thought it was funny. I explained there was no reason for her to do it. It was under-cutting Polly. Linda kept insisting it was funny and she was going to continue doing it. I told her to stop it. Her lips began to quiver and she told me she was going to do it no matter what I said. I lost it. I told her that if she continued I would kill her. Stagehands grabbed me before I could reach her. My career on Alice was over and we all knew it. I had better get the fuck out of there. I went upstairs, packed up my office, got in my car and drove to Palm Springs. When I reached the desert, I be- gan to scream "Free At Last! Free at Last!" I didn't even go back for the wrap-up party. D'Angelo, Ray and Harvey were fired after the first season. We all lost a fortune on that series. FLASHFOR-WARD! Two years ago, Linda Lavin came to Palm Springs to do her singing act. I said what the hell and went to see her. After the performance (and she was really good) she saw me and hugged and kissed me. She also told everyone in the crowd that I was "the best writer she ever worked with."

CHAPTER FOURTEEN

THE VELVET KNIFE STRIKES

ONE DAY DURING ALICE I PICKED UP THE TRADES ONE morning and became very angry and pissed off. There was an article say- ing that Doug Cramer was doing a Movie of the Week for ABC which they were going to use as a spin-off for a possible series. It was called "LOVE BOAT". I immediately called Gordon Farr at the Newhart show and asked if he had seen the article? He had and was as upset as I was. Remember, we had gone to Doug in 1973-4 and pitched him our Love Boat. He had passed on it ex- plaining that it was too soon after Love American had aired. It was natural for us – once Irv Wilson couldn't sell it for us to try Cramer. We had done lots of projects for him and had a good relationship with Doug. For a while we were 'his boys.' The arti- cle went on to 'explain' that he had bought the rights to the book

"The Love Boat" by a former social director on a cruise ship. Hey, co- incidences happen but what was he trying to pull? Why didn't he call us and explain the situation or even ask us to do the project for him. Did he think we were going to let him get away with this? Doug had formed a partnership with Aaron Spelling on the project. Spelling was the most successful packager of TV shows at the time. We called Bernie Brillstein (who remembered the whole thing) and he got us a lawyer. Our lawyer called Cramer who insisted that we had never come to him with our version.

That was total bullshit! He said we were lying about pitching it to him. I thought it was time to play 'hard ball.' We went through depositions and I could sense that Doug blamed me for all this trouble. He believed I was the instigator not Gordon. Our lawyer, who was a young guy at the time, (he subsequently became one of the toughest attorneys in the business) to us that it was a 'he says... he says' kind of law suit and might take years to get to court. If we wanted to stop production, we'd have to get really tough and sue ABC and warned that if ABC got pissed at us they might never want to do business with us again. I called Andy Segal, who was no longer at ABC and asked if he remembered when Gordy and I pitched "Love Boat" to him? He said of course he did. He even had a note in his files about our pitch. I was for going ahead with our lawsuit but everyone else was getting nerv- ous and when Cramer offered a small settlement, I asked Gor- don, Brillstein and the attorney what they thought we should do? They all said they thought we should take the crappy deal. I re- luctantly agreed. What a mistake that was. We should have con- tinued with our lawsuit against Cramer, Spelling and ABC. Had we prevailed we would have made millions. Not only was "LOVE BOAT" a huge success but one of the biggest selling series in syndication. It is still on the air every night. After the settlement Gordon and Lynne Farr were hired as Producers of Love Boat for all the years it was on the air. I got a small cash settlement. In hindsight I was an idiot and shouldn't have let everyone talk me into what I knew was wrong.

Arnold Kane, became persona non grata that day forward at the Spelling Company and Mr. Cramer. He swore to people that he 'would get me'. I don't know about that but he did cost me lots of money and jobs through the years. Gordon did very well and eventually sued Spelling for his share of profits and after many years won the suit. (Some suspicious type friends have always suspected that Gordo getting the job on "Love Boat" and Brillstein's advice to settle the lawsuit was a conspiracy. Gord and Brillstein had a deal already in hand when they urged me not to continue with our suit...Brillstein knew he would be collecting his commissions on Farr's new gig and he also took 10% of my cash settlement. I don't have any proof on this but it seems a tad coincidental. As you will find out later in this book – Bernie Brillstein almost ruined my life many times.

CHAPTER FIFTEEN

YOU CAN'T GO HOME AGAIN

IN THE SPRING OF 1977 SAM DENOFF WAS OFFERED A New York series owned by David Susskind called "ON OUR OWN". Sam asked me to do it with him and I accepted. I hadn't been back in NYC since I had left in 1968. There were no offers imminent for me in Hollywood and I liked the pilot a lot. Working with Sam was icing on the cake. Before we left, Sam and I wrote new scenes for the pilot introducing new characters we felt the series needed. We were going to re-shoot the pilot and it would air as our first episode. We also did some casting for these new characters.

It felt strange going back to what had been my home for most of my life, but a place that I had no feelings for. My parents had moved to Florida and I didn't really have any friends left. An- other benefit would be working with my pal Alan Wagner once again. Alan was now head of development at CBS in New York. My living arrangements were taken care of when a friend intro- duced me to a young actress who wanted to move to L.A. We just switched apartments. Melody's was on Central Park South so I know I got the best of our arrangement. Susskind's company was putting Sam up in a hotel on CPS. The idea of working with Susskind was also a plus. He had been a TV legend for many years. NYC was hot as hell when we arrived. Sam's suite at the hotel Navarro was just 3 blocks from mine. We set up offices at CBS's production building on West 57th Street. Basically all of CBS news programs came from that site. The building and crews weren't geared up for a comedy. Our production and stage crews were still doing the Walter Cronkite Show and 60 Minutes. It was wild to see Cronkite and Mike Wallace wondering the halls.

"ON OUR OWN" had been created by Bob Randall, one of the sweetest men I had ever met in my life. Bob hadn't done any television writing prior to writing the pilot. He was a playwright and had just finished a best-selling mystery/suspense book "The Fan." That man could just plain write. That was our complete staff. Just Denoff, Bob and me. Bob had no problem being the low man on the totem pole. He freely admitted he knew 'bubkis' about TV writing and was willing to learn. Did he ever. The three of us became inseparable. Randall has recently gone through a divorce. His wife announced on day that she was leaving him for another woman. Bob was a wickedly, funny, talented homosex- ual. Soon after we got acquainted Bob went into Sam's office, then mine to say that he was gay and that he hoped we wouldn't mind working with him. We, of course, told him certainly not. That, coming from

Hollywood a large percentage of our friends were gay. Besides, it was none of our damn business. Bob Ran- dall was a very special person in my life until he died from AIDS a few years ago. I was lucky to have had him as a friend.

"On Our Own" was the story of two young women working in an advertising agency. They were literally 'on their own' for the first time in their lives. The cast was excellent. Bess Armstrong and Lennie Green were the young stars. They hadn't really done anything before the series. Bess was really good and went on to have a successful career in Hollywood. Lennie went onto be- come a director later in life. Among the other performers was Gretchen Wyler who played their tough boss, Gretchen. She had worked for me on "Pantomime Quiz" and was a major star on B'Way. The actress that knocked our socks off was Dixie Carter. Dixie played the elegant office tramp and was brilliantly hysteri- cal. Dixie was the only actor I ever met who didn't want her part enlarged. She had a few show-stopping speeches each show and didn't want to screw with what was working. Dixie had just divorced her wealthy stockbroker husband and lived in a 15-room penthouse apartment on 5th Avenue with her two adorable daughters. She drove around NYC in a chauffeured limousine. It was wild. Dixie married the great actor Hal Holbrook and they remained close friends of mine until Dixie passed away a couple of years ago.

Susskind was the Executive Producer and packager of the series. He was one of the most successful producers in televi- sion and movie history. For some strange reason David and Sam got to be enemies during the series which was too bad. Susskind would arrive at the Studio on Fridays a little bombed and he and Sam would begin arguing. In spite of that for the first thirteen weeks on the air our show was one of CBS' few hits. The head of CBS New York was an idiot named Harvey Sheppard. He was an expert research and statistical expert - you know the kind of guy who wore pens in his jacket pocket. Harvey was about as funny as a hemorrhoid. He proved that when he moved to Los Angeles to head up all of television. He is remembered as saying, "Comedy on TV is dead!" He is also remembered for dropping CBS into third place in the network ratings. I have no idea where is now - maybe selling storm windows? On show night Alan Wag- ner and his family would show up and laugh their brains out. Harvey and Mrs. Sheppard would attend and unless she elbowed him he wouldn't know a joke had just been said. He also wore the worst toupee in the world. Harvey would have been thrown out of funerals for depressing the mourners. Since he hated com- edies he kept moving "On Our Own" on the schedule so viewers never knew when it was on. He killed the series. What a damned fool!!!!

About three weeks after our arrival in NYC a funny thing happened. I was having dinner with two old friends when the lights went out. I knew immediately that it was a blackout having lived through an earlier one in the 60's. I left the restaurant, walked home, climbed the stairs to my apartment and sent to bed. Obviously the elevators weren't working. In the morning there was still no electricity and like a fool I walked to the office ready for work. The security guard at CBS looked at me like I was deranged as I headed to our offices. It hadn't occurred to me that my electric typewriter was of no use. (Yes, these were the days before computers.) I finally called Denoff and told him that I was coming over to his hotel and that we'd work there. "No stinkin' blackout is gonna stop our re-write." On the way over I figured out that I might need a candle since I was going to have to hike up to his suite. Typical of New Yorkers in an emergency the shop keepers were gouging citizens who needed to buy things. You think $10 was too much to pay for a lousy fifty cent candle? I arrived at The Navarro and began to climb the stairs to Sam's suite...and climb and climb and climb. Twenty-two floors later I weakly knocked on his door with my tongue hanging out and collapsed on his couch. I promptly fell asleep and that ended our re-write. Sam's suite was next door to Liv Ullman's. That in- credible looking Swedish actress was starring on Broadway at the time in a musical version of "I Remember Momma". Sam would stand outside her door and coo to her in what he thought sounded Swedish throwing around the word "herring" a lot. Liv never opened her door. Maybe she didn't like herring.

It was during "On Our Own" that I met one of the strangest human beings I had ever encountered – Andrew Smith. Andrew was a writer and a good one. He was also a male model and a boxer. I think he had one professional fight using the name "Kid Natural". He also played the tuba. How many boxers have you ever hear of that played the tuba? Come on think. Andrew fell in love with Bess Armstrong and they had a torrid love affair for years. It finally ended because 'Kid Natural' was even too crazy for Beth. He's still living in New York, is married and has a child. For a few years he worked on Barbara Walter's 'The View' on ABC. Someday someone will write Andrew's story but it'll proba- bly sold as Science Fiction. I love the guy and we still talk all the time.

Weekends were becoming a problem for me. I would fly back to Palm Springs on some of them. I'd fly to Bermuda every once in a while. I was terrible lonely in NYC. I wasn't looking for- ward to the coming fall and winter and the lousy weather. Hallie Stitch flew in for a weekend and it was wonderful seeing her. The truth is although I like "On Our Own" a lot I missed the desert. Susskind's business affairs person had made a big mistake and hadn't taken an option on my services after thirteen shows so I was free to go. By that time I had pitched a few comedy TV ideas to Alan Wagner at CBS and he bought them which gave me something to do when I got home. After the weekend I spent with Hallie I missed the hell out of her and wanted to live together with her in Palm Springs. When I flew out and got to my condo in the Springs she wasn't there. She finally called and in a strange voice told me that she wasn't going to meet me. When I asked why, she replied that she was going to Las Vegas to get married. I dropped the phone. Married? To who? It seems she had met this guy at a party in L.A. and they decided to get married. I asked her if that meant 'the blowjob' that weekend for me was out of the question? I was in total shock and hung up. No sooner had I hung up than Carlinda called. She and Hallie were roommates and that she was driving down to be with me. She drove down and when I asked why Hallie would do something so crazy. Carly explained that Hallie had been working around the clock at her new job at ABC and had gotten a little weird. No shit.

When I flew back to New York, after the weekend, every- one was very solicitous to me. However, I was more determined than ever to get back to California. Maybe subconsciously I blamed the series that had forced me to NYC for what happened to Hallie and me. I felt terrible for Sam Denoff when Bob Randall decided to leave at the same time but we helped him put together a writing staff which included Andrew Smith. CBS tried to get me to stay.

Alan Wagner offered me 'guaranteed' pilots and other induce-ments. Susskind, because of his attitude toward Sam of- fered me lots of money and other perks, but I turned them down. (Another questionable decision by me). After I got back to Cali- fornia David Susskind would call me at home to say if the series was picked-up he'd move it to L.A. and wanted me produce it without Sam. Because of Harvey Sheppard's screwing around with the schedule "On Our Own" dropped in the rating and was cancelled after one season. It was a good series and deserved a better fate. The cast threw a lovely going-away-party for Randall and me and presented us with fabulous gifts in appreciation of our work.

It doesn't take a rocket scientist to see a pattern in my busi-ness career as well as my relationship with women. I seemed to be uncomfortable with commitments of any type, be they per-sonal or career. That took the form of leaving TV series rather than remain with them. The grass was always greener to me on the next show offered. If I had my professional life to live over again, I would pay more attention to the business part of my ca- reer. I would have chosen the projects I did more carefully. It wasn't smart of me to get so emotionally involved with a series and doing them with friends. Now that I'm retired, my WGA pen- sion was affective big time by my poor business decisions. An- other prob-lem I had was that integrity, honesty and loyalty were very import-ant to me. I trusted too many 'friends' who weren't friends at all.

Socially I was known as a 'great date' but didn't expect an-ything more serious. (A feeling that worked for me.) That I never equated alone with loneliness. I enjoyed my time by myself. I never felt that I need people around to make me happy. Deep analyses finally straightened my ass out.

CHAPTER SIXTEEN

HERE WE GO AGAIN

I WAS HAPPY TO BE BACK 'HOME' AND BEFORE BEGIN-
ning my two pilots for CBS I went to Los Angeles to visit a friend
working at the Columbia/Warner Brothers lot. While there I
bumped into Rob Reiner and Phil Mishkin who had begun writing together. "ALL IN THE FAMILY" had finally ended its brilliant run and Rob wanted to concentrate on writing. I had not met
Mishkin before. Rob asked what I was doing and I told him that
I had a couple of pilot scripts to write but otherwise I was taking
it easy. Rob and Phil had created a new series and the ubiquitous
Fred Silverman, now running ABC had bought it. Silverman
changed networks more than a hooker changed underwear. Rob
was to star in the, as well as Executive Produce it. They asked if I
would be inter- ested in doing the show with them? I told them
honestly that I really just wanted to write my projects and get some

sun. They asked if they could send the script to me in Palm Spring to read. Sure. The next day a driver from Columbia knocked on my door and handed me their script. I figured what the hell, I'd read it and then call and say, "Thanks but no thanks." The series was called "FREE COUNTRY". It was the story of a Jewish immigrant family that had just come over to America in the early 1900's. It was the story of Rob's grandfather – Carl Reiner's father and Rob's grandmother. The boys came up with the clever idea to open and close each story. The 'old man' now in his 90's (also played by Rob) would start to tell a story and they would dissolve back to him and his wife as young adults trying to make a life for themselves in America. At the end of each show, they'd dissolve back to the old man who would close the show. In other words each story was book-ended by Rob as this old curmudgeon. I read the script and flipped out. It may have been the best TV script I'd ever read - Funny, sad and passionate. It made you care deeply about those young immigrants. Shaking my head I called Rob and told him, "You got me." I decided to put my own two pilots for CBS on hold. Rob Reiner was one of the best writers and men I've ever worked with. He's now a brilliant movie director and owns his own production company Castle Rock.

Doing the series with Rob was an absolute ball. He's un- believably creative while at the same time unbelievably volatile. The series had been picked up for five episodes and we began writing the other four scripts immediately. Hold it! Let's think about that for a second. How the fuck can any series hope to make it when it's picked up for only five shows? Never happen. We hired a young writer Sy Rosen to work with us. Sy was very talented and went on to have a good career. While we were writ- ing, casting having sets built and opening titles designed we got some WILD news. Crazy Fred Silverman left ABC to take over NBC. What did I say about this nutcase? Two young people named Marcy Carsey and Tom Werner took over the network. They were bright and eager but didn't have a clue about what to do with this "Jewish Immigrant" series. It was a hold-over from the Silverman regime. Free Country made Tom and Marcy very nervous. ABC was having success with programming like "Happy Days" and "LaVerne & Shirley". A series about some- one's grandfather didn't quite blend in – but they were stuck with the commitment. Rob Reiner was a very sought-after talent and it didn't make any sense for a network to piss him off by cancel- ling a creation of his before it even began.

One of the first things I did was insist that Phil Mishkin not work in our offices. Phil was a neurotic, high-strung fella... who would have made all of us basket cases. At the time, he was living in his office at Columbia having been thrown out of his house by his wife. Get the picture? Being a very disciplined pro- ducer, I knew Phil and I would kill each other. Both he and Rob under- stood my concerns. When Phil had written pages he would send them over by messenger. Strangely the system worked out fine. Mishkin, of course would come to the tapings, but I just didn't want a distraction during the week. When Tom Werner heard that I had agreed to do the series he called me and thanked me a lot. He, also, begged me to keep Rob pacified. ABC was afraid of Rob's temper. Tom then said, "Arnie, you and ABC are going to do a lot of business together. I owe you big time." Remember that. Having a network indebted to you is something all writer/ producers wish for.

Rob had a very specific vision of the series which made it unusual. Most taped shows are front lit and have no shadows like real life. The sets are just bright. He hired a Broadway lighting expert to come in a 'design' a look. We actually shot the shows in sepia tones. It was gorgeous. I have never seen that look since. The sets were extraordinary. You could almost 'smell' and 'taste' the lower East Side of New York. The costumes looked like they were bought off pushcarts. They were perfect. Of all the series I've done "Free Country" was the best looking production. We would meet at around 8:30 a.m and begin writing before Rob had to go to rehearsal. We worked our asses off in the few hours we had each morning. We'd meet after rehearsal and continue scribing. It was one of the most enjoyable writing experiences of my life. ABC, however, didn't really like the show and began mov- ing it around its schedule just to play the 5 episodes off. What a tragedy. I enjoyed every minute of my time with Reiner. There was noth- ing he couldn't do well.

Werner and Carsey were in an untenable position. They couldn't blame the series on Silverman as he was at NBC. They weren't about to make Rob the heavy not if they wanted to do business with him again. It's one of the facts of life in show busi- ness that new heads of studios or networks hate to get involved with the previous administrations deals. If the project is a big hit they will take credit for it, but if not they immediately start look- ing for someone to blame. "Hey, don't blame us for this piece of shit, we didn't buy it.

After "Free Country" was cancelled I stated writing my CBS pilots. I, also, asked Bernie Brillstein to call Tom Werner and set up a 'development' breakfast. I wanted to see just how much the network "still wanted to do lots of business with me." Strike while the iron's hot, right? Tom was very happy to see me and while we were eating our eggs and bagels we chatted about everything under the sun. I have already pleaded 'guilty' to not play the Hollywood game very well and being totally honest when asked my opinion. Oh, Lord, why didn't I ever learn!? Tom finally asked, "What did I REALLY think of Free Country?" Even a dwarf in denial would have picked up on that when he said REALLY THINK? He obviously wanted me to knock the hell out of the show. He wanted a negative response. Either not picking up on the nuance of this question or not giving a shit, I blurted out that I was never so proud of a series in my life. A cream-cheese-iron curtain descended over Tom's face. When I asked if we should finally talk 'business', he quickly made some lame excuse about a meeting, and left the restaurant. I even got stuck with the lousy bill. After that disaster I never did business with Marcy and Werner again. Oh, by the way, they eventually became independent producers and owned things like the Bill Cosby Show, Roseanne, etc. They are trillionaires. On the few occasions that Tom and I met after he left the network, he was very friendly but I guess I'm still the SCHMUCK for not telling him what he wanted to hear. That's not true. I would have hated myself for lying and kissing ass.

I wrote my pilots for CBS. Alan Wagner liked them but they were never shot. While doing a few odd scripts for different people I decided to buy another home. My apartment was great but I felt like putting down some roots. After months of looking I finally saw this bachelor house in the Hollywood Hills. I wanted to spend the rest of my life in it. It had a spectacular view of the City and terrific pool area behind the house. All my friends were doing fine.

Gordon and Lynne were producing "Love Boat", Bruce Johnson was producing a series for Gary Marshall, David Yarnell had a few things going. Bill D'Angelo, Ray Allen and Harvey Bullock were doing some kid's series for Silverman at NBC, Sam Denoff has just returned from New York and my old Buddy Duke Vincent had become Aaron Spelling's partner. Aaron, fell in love with Duke and decided that he needed a tough, confident Italian, with him. That started a partnership that lasted for years and years. Duke was born with a golden Cannelloni in his mouth. I still see him and talk to him every week.

In 1978 Dave Yarnell was asked to produce two Comedy Roasts that 20th Century Fox was doing for ABC late night. He asked me to write and produce the Roasts with him. The first Roast was for O.J. Simpson. I used to see O.J. at a popular res-taurant on Pico Blvd that was frequented by sports personalities. "The Juice" had just retired from pro football and hung out there. He was usually in the company of a beautiful blonde. He was still married at the time but he and Nicole were inseparable. I got to know both of them after they married and bought a beach house next to the Denoffs in Laguna Beach. At that point O.J. was one of the most popular celebrities in the world. We produced the Roast at the Riviera Hotel in La Vegas. The panel roasting O.J. consisted of every famous athlete and comedian around. The dais was like a Who's Who of Comedy Howard Cosell was our host. Writing the Roast was like re-visiting my stand-up days. The material could be funny, rough, hostile and angry – but all in good natured fun. During the show O.J. took the barbs thrown at him very well and delivered his 'answers' brilliantly. It was so refresh- ing to be able to write hard comedy without worrying about a story. The second

Roast was for Monty Hall. We produced it at ABC studios in Los Angeles. Danny Thomas was the host and our dais was filled with top comedians and television stars. It was very funny and Monty was a good sport about it.

Kim LeMasters, who I had first met at Warner Brothers during "Alice" had moved over to CBS. Kim was a very bright guy and we became really good friends. He and his wife Donna and I would go out a lot because we enjoyed each other's company. Kim became a loyal friend at the network and always saw to it that I had a script development deal. Bless his heart. When he became President of CBS Television he never forgot his pal, Arnie. Like many television executives Kim had a certain arro- gance. Some people couldn't wait for Kim to fail and when he did they kicked dirt all over him. All I know is he was a loyal friend to me and a bright guy.

In 1979 Universal Television decided to get into comedy in a big way. They began to sign comedy writer/producers including Sam Denoff. Universal called Brillstein and signed a develop- ment deal with me. I had never had an exclusive deal with any- one before. I was used to jumping from deal to deal. Universal quickly flew me to NYC knowing that Alan Wagner was a fan. He made a quick script deal with me. The Universal bigwigs liked that I had a friend at one of the networks. They didn't like spend- ing money on creative people unless there was a guaranteed payoff. I immediately called Carlinda and hired her as my secre- tary and started writing my pilot script. Midway through it Wagner called and told me to stop. The 'shmendrick' Harvey Sheppard had decided that the New York office couldn't develop any more projects with West Coast writers anymore. CBS paid Universal off for my abandoned script but I wasn't very happy sitting around on my duff Sam Denoff was fooling around with a few things when the studio pitched NBC a series based on a Thorne Smith novella called "TURNABOUT". Smith was a fascinating Cana- dian writer who created unusual stories based on fantasy themes/ Among his famous creations are "Topper" and "I Married a Witch." "Turnabout" had been developed the year before, but the script needed lots of help. (Here he goes again) Fred Silver- man insisted that Sam Denoff take the project over. "Turnabout" deals with a husband and wife who switch bodies. Sam and Michael Rhodes re-did the script and Silverman ordered a pilot. If the pilot sold I was to become the show's writer/producer. Rhodes had been an agent and was then one of the top producers on the Universal lot.

As part of the NBC order Silverman insisted that John Shuck play the husband (who is really the wife in the husband's body.) Fred liked John's work in other NBC series. The tricky part was casting the wife (who really was the husband in his wife's body.) Sound confusing? IT WAS! Imagine how the viewers felt trying to watch the series? Universal sent all their contract ac- tresses up for the role. No established actress would touch the series. One of those young contract actresses was SHARON GLESS. Sharon has just finished as a regular on the "Switch" TV series. When all these actresses met with Sam and Michael and they explained the series the girls ran out of the office and joined a nunnery. Everyone who met Sharon Gless adored her and wanted her for the part. She was leery about doing it not having done 'comedy' before. She was finally talked into it – thank God. The pilot was shot and NBC ordered six episodes.

This is a good point to point out that, years earlier a TV series was always bought for 26 shows. That gave it a chance to 'find' an audience or allowed the audience to 'find' it. The number of shows ordered reduced over the years and usually a show was ordered for 13 episodes. Unfortunately, as I've stated before new series are ordered for as little as 4, 5 or six episodes. That means the series has to become an instant hit or most likely can- celled before an audience even knew it was on the air. It's an unfair pressure to make it quickly. If this process had been in existence – earlier series such as: "ALL IN THE FAMILY", "THE DICK VAN DYKE SHOW" and "MARY TYLER MOORE", and other greats would have been stillborn. Back to "Turnabout". In order to try and bring some semblance of sanity to this confusing, but intriguing premise we decided to keep the device Thorne Smith had come up with in his novel to change the husband and wife's identity. At a garage sale they picked up an ugly statue of Buddha, which has magical powers unbeknownst to them. That night they got into a dumb argument about "you have it easy. I'd switch places with you in a second, etc " The Buddha began to glow and 'switched them.'

To illustrate the 'switch' Sam came up with a brilliant com- edy piece. When the husband (now in his wife's body) got up in the middle of the night to 'pee' "he" goes into the bathroom, stands in front of the toilet and we hear a loud scream as he no- tices he's 'missing' something. It was a great joke and helped explain what happened to our couple. We put together a small writing staff consisting of Ken Hecht who had worked for me on "Make Your Own Kind of Music" and two women writers Barbara Corday and Barbara Avedon...Sharon Gless was BRILLIANT in the part of the husband trapped in the body of his wife. She has the guts of a bandit and learned to smoke big cigars every time the 'wife' was alone. It was a baffling and muddled show to write

– the wife is really the....and the husband is really the....I'm getting a migraine just thinking about it. John Shuck did a really good job in his confusing part as well. The one constant was Sharon's fabulous performance. Corday and Avedon had developed a television series, before joining Turnabout, involving two female police officers. When they met Gless they realized they had found their 'Chris Cagney' for "Cagney and Lacy". To cut to the chase: Turnabout never had a chance on the air. Lousy time slot and very confusing premise. Gless and I had dinner together all the time it would have been very easy to get romantically involved with her. She was gorgeous, funny, bright and single. We remain close friends and talk all the time. In fact, when Sharon got mar- ried-yearslatertoBarbaraCorday'sex-husbandBarney Rosenzweig she threw me her bridal bouquet after the wedding. When NBC knew they weren't picking up 'Turnabout' they asked Sam Denoff and me to create a comedy pilot for Gless. The schmuck Silverman had been fired and the new executives didn't want her to slip away to another network. We wrote some- thing very funny that everyone liked but it involved shooting be- fore a studio audience. Sharon had never worked before an au- dience before and was too frightened to try it. (now she's an ac- complished theater actress and has won many awards.) She would have been brilliantly funny in the part we wrote, but it was another of those 'close but no cigar' events. Corday and Ave- don's "Cagney & Lacy" went on CBS starring Gless and Tyne Daley and became a monster hit winning Emmy's for both actresses. Both Barbara's made lot of money on the series. Rosenzweig became the series' Executive Producer.

Corday de- cided after Cagney & Lacy became such a huge hit to give up writing and became a network executive.

Ken Hecht went on to produce many other series. During Turnabout, before it was cancelled, I got a call from Ray Allen who asked me to do him a favor. Could I hire Bill D'Angelo to direct an episode. Bill wasn't doing anything and Ray wanted to help his old partner. I was happy to hire Bill and typically "Nero" showed up on the set with an entourage. We all teased the hell out of him for that. You will notice an interesting pattern that has formed. The same names seem to crop up again and again. Yar- nell, Denoff, Persky, Gordy Farr, Bruce Johnson, Duke Vincent, Bill D'Angelo, Ray Allen Sharon Gless Corday, Kim Lemasters, Fred Silverman, Doug Cramer, Carlinda, Hallie, Ken Hecht, Ber- nie Brillstein,etc. It only goes to show what a small business it really is and was. At times I almost felt incestuous. My dear friend Ray Allen became ill with cancer and had to retire. Ray and his girlfriend, Pat, would drive over to my house every day and Ray would sit in my Jacuzzi. The hot water seemed to ease his pain. I was never so unhappy in my life when he finally died. He was the first friend I had that had died which made me very angry and as often happens moments of anger fed by depression. A day doesn't go by that I don't think of Ray Allen.

A writer's strike was looming which didn't make any of us happy. The WGA's record when it came to striking against the studios and networks was pitiful. The Guild would throw picket lines up, make lots of noise and then they would settle the strike without winning any important benefits for the members. While I was trying to come up with some creative excuse why I could n't carrying a picket sign once the strike was called, Alan Rafkin phoned. I got to know Alan when he directed an episode of Bridget Loves Bernie and a few Alice's. Rafkin had become Executive Producer and director of "ONE DAY AT A TIME" a hit series for CBS. Alan was an actor's director. They enjoyed working with him because he was funny and knew his stuff. He also had a ploy especially when the actors began to misbehave or a producer started giving him hard time. Alan threw great tantrums. They usually got everyone's attention. I had known Alan for so long that I could predict one of his tantrums before he thought of it. "One Day at A Time" had been on the air for years and seemed to get getting 'tired'. This can happen on any long running series, especially if the staff remains the same. He thought that the show needed some new blood and offered me the job as "Creative Consultant'. My job was to look over the stories they had devel- oped, try to save some scripts that the show had abandoned, write a few scripts myself and breathe some life into the series. Not only did the job offer come in handy but they were going to pay me big bucks.

The series was a strange one. The cast didn't seem to hang out together very much. Bonnie Franklin was the star and was a nice enough woman but very private. No one knew where she lived. Scripts and re-writes were handed to her manager to take to Bonnie. I had never heard of that before or since. Valerie Bertinelli was not only a great actress but a warm nice young woman. Pat Harrington, who was the 'super' of their building, and I go back a long way. He was a funny actor and he worked for me on Pantomime Quiz in the 50's. He welcomed me with open arms. I don't know if Rafkin had done a big job selling me but they expected me to help the series big time. I hope I didn't disappoint them. Bonnie even tried to fix me up with a couple of her girlfriends. It was obvious that the biggest problem the show had was that the writing staff was very white bread. Which is unusual for a comedy show. During the writing sessions there was no kibitzing or laughing when we met. The writing Executive Producers were like insurance salesmen, "White Bread City." However no one could knock the job I was doing. I helped re-write scripts and wrote two original stories that were totally unlike an- ything the series had tried before. In fact, the executives of Nor- mal Lear's company who owned the series became fans and indicated they need me the next season. It felt great to be appre- ciated again. We finished up the season and waited for the up- coming writer's strike and hoped it wouldn't last long. I was sup- posed to rejoin "One Day At A Time", but as a Producer.

CHAPTER SEVENTEEN

A BIG WHITE LIE!

THE WRITERS GUILD HAS DONE WONDERFUL WORK getting their membership things like basic minimums and excellent health and dental benefits for their members. But there seems to be some- thing wrong to me about a creative person belonging to a union. I don't want to demean honest working people but unions always brought up images of hard hats and Jimmy Hoffa. My opinion probably doesn't make sense but there it is. Does somebody who writes funny things really need a union?

One of the problems that became apparent before the WGA went on strike in 1980 was that a small but very loud group of members wanted to strike at any cost. They behaved like they had never met an honest or fair boss in their lives. Executives were bloodsuckers and fascists to these left-wing radicals. I heard them use those words. Sadly, a small group of these men and women seemed to be controlling the negotiations with man- agement. Another problem was that the vast majority of mem- bership of the WGA were freelance writers and weren't able to make a living at their craft. That remains true today. Over 80% of the Guild are unemployed. Television series had started putting together large writing staffs and were doing almost all the scripts in house. These writers also took credit as producers which made them "hyphen- ates". Check out the credits of your favorite series and see what I mean. You will see a chorus line of pro- ducers. The biggest prob- lem the WGA had and continues to have is that it represents two different memberships. The free- lance writer and hyphenates. Hyphenates are the real power in television. They create, write and produce the series. Free-lance writers have gone the way of the Lava lamp. Studios and net- works couldn't care less of some man or woman writing one or two scripts a year. In 1980 the trou- blemakers wanting to strike were generally made up of free-lance writers. They had nothing to lose by striking, they weren't working anyway. While negotia- tions continued the Guild formed picket lines around studios. A few of us refused to walk those picket lines. We were in show business for crying out loud not the Teamsters. In order not to get fined we would call in sick. I claimed to have a severe case of the heartbreak of psoriasis and Bruce Johnson we was going in for a hysterectomy.

Bruce would come over to my house every day while we lounged at my pool and tried to think of movie ideas but gener- ally just hung around and schmoozed. We both had friends on man- agement's negotiating team who wanted to end the strike as badly as we did. Unless production began no one was making any money. Bruce and I kept hearing a settlement was near, but then some hothead in the WGA negotiating group would begin to rant and rave and insult management and any offer that was on the table would be pulled. The Guild's membership was una- ware of what was taking place.

They just heard that those 'lousy' bosses were at fault. Bruce hated not working even more than I did. We were both frustrated while getting a good suntan at my pool so we decided to goose things along. The damn strike was going on for months. Enough! Now, you have to promise that you won't tell a soul about what I'm going to reveal. This is all true. I called a member of the Board of the WGA, named Irma Kalish and told her that we had just had a meeting at my home with about 30 of the most important hyphenates in TV and that "We were sick and tired of the antics of the members of our negotiating committee. That if the Board didn't call them off we were prepared to take full-page ads out in the Trade papers denouncing the strike and saying we were going to cross the picket lines and go back to work. That enough was enough. Bruce who was on an extension phone con- firmed everything I said to Irma. She panicked and told us we couldn't do something like that, it would ruin everything. I firmly told her that "I couldn't control the guys anymore. They were adamant about the strike ending." Bruce and I were wearing bathing suits while this conversation took place. Poor Irma was convinced we meant what we had said. She said she was going to immediately inform Frank Pierson, the President of the Guild. We hung up and laughed thinking it was the end of our little joke. We just wanted to shake things up because we were bored out of our skulls. Later that evening I got a phone call from Frank Pierson asking if he could meet with the group of hyphenates. I informed Frank that the group didn't want to meet with anyone. They just wanted the lousy strike to end and get back to work. It had gone on too long as it was. He asked if we could give him 24-hours before we acted on our threat to take the ads out. I agreed saying I could probably hold them for 24-hours but that was it.

The WGA strike ended the next day. Pierson called again to thank me for all my help. This is the first time that anyone knows the real reason the 1980 WGA strike was settled. It's an absolutely and true story. Sorry Irma Kalish.

CHAPTER EIGHTEEN

BACK IN THE SADDLE AGAIN

EVERYONE HUSTLED BACK TO WORK. I WAS TOLD THAT "One Day At A Time" indeed wanted me back but not as a producer liked they promised but as Creative Consultant. I told them to fuck off. Ken Hecht and his new partner Bob Brunner just signed a deal as Executive Producers of "PRIVATE BENJAMIN" for CBS. It had been a very successful movie starring Goldie Hawn. They asked if I would like to join them as one of their producers and I accepted. I jumped at the opportunity of working with a friend again. All, my career, it seemed I'd rather work with friends on 'iffy' shows than on a possible hit series. It was a stupid practice but one I was comfortable with. At least I knew I would enjoy coming to work in the morning. "Private Benjamin" was in its second season but was a troubled show. Ken and Bob put together a good staff including Arnold Margolin, one of the creators of Love American Style. Margolin got the short end of the stick. He had to work with the actors on the set while we sat in the office writing a re-writing. Alan Shayne was still running Warner Brothers TV and was frantic about the low ratings on the series. Lorna Patterson, who played Benjamin, refused to play a "Jewish Princess" which of course was the whole idea of the story. A kosher fish out of water. She insisted on playing the role straight. She didn't realize that 'straight' wasn't funny...the whole premise of the movie was gone. Why didn't Shayne fire her? A good question with no answer. She should have been sent back to the unemployment line. But, believe it or not Eileen Brennen, who played Benjamin's officer and main antagonist, was the chief culprit. Eileen had mor- phed into an uncontrollable, neurotic powder-keg ready explode at any moment. Turned out she was doing drugs and we never knew which Brennan would come out of her dressing room. It could be the pleasant, smiling Eileen or the off-the-wall Eileen.

Poor Arnold Margolin had to suffer though her abusive behavior. He should have received hazard pay. Alan Shayne would sit in the screening room looking at the dailies and literally weep. In- stead of insisting she went into rehab he would shut his eyes to the problem and hope for a miracle. Remember he was the same Alan Shayne I had problems with on "Alice".

Well, when you hope enough – Margolin was an L.A. Deputy Sheriff in his spare time and had receive a call telling him that Eileen had been hit by a car the night before and had been injured seriously. She had been having dinner with Goldie Hawn and was complaining about how terrible the series was and how she was working with a bunch of incompetent fools. As they left the restaurant Brennan stepped between parked cars and was struck. The hospital report was that she was going to live but was out of the series. I rushed to the office and put up an empty coffee can with a sign printed on it, "Defense Fund for the Driver Who Hit Eileen." It was a sick joke but everyone on the staff, lots of crew and even members of the cast dropped money into the can. One of her co-stars put in his American Express card. We had three more episodes left in the season when Shayne had the brilliant idea of bringing Polly Holliday in to replace Brennan. Polly wasn't sure she wanted to do it, but when she heard I was part of the staff and would be her 'friend' in court she accepted the offer. The real reason was that Warner's probably parked a Brink's truck up to her front door. It was nice seeing POLLY again and I knew she'd be fabulous playing a Flo-like officer which would have been a natural. Polly was better playing those parts than anyone alive. Hold it! At our first meeting she told me that she was not going to play a "Flo" character but would play it straight. Why Shayne didn't have it in her contract is beyond me. I told Polly that straight wasn't funny, but she insisted. She was okay not really good as the officer. The three episodes ran out and the shows were lousy. CBS cancelled Benjamin and to her credit Polly apologized to me and admitted she'd been wrong.

On March 4, 1982 I went to Bernie Brillstein's office to talk to him and make a few phone calls. John Belushi, one of his big- gies was in an office using the phone. We waved to each other and he went on with his call. He looked awful and it was obvious he was in bad shape. He looked as if he hadn't slept in days. Everyone in town knew that Belushi had a big drug problem but no one was willing to confront him about it and force him to get clean. The next day, I found out John had died from an overdose in his cabin at The Chateau Marmont. It was a tragedy! Brillstein told me later that Belushi had come into his office and asked him for five-thousand dollars in cash. His excuse was that he was going to buy one of Les Paul's original guitars. A lie and that he was really going to use the money to buy drugs. Bernie gave it to him. He also claimed that he felt guilty about it because in hindsight he contributed to John's death. The truth is that Brill- stein and John's agents at CAA never tried to help the guy. They ignored John's problem because they were making too much money from him. If they had confronted him Belushi would have fired them so they took the easy way out. They closed their eyes to Belushi being a junkie. The disgusting fact is that studio, pro- duction companies, agents and managers allowed the drug prob- lem to grow until it became an epidemic in the industry. The al- mighty dollar seemed more important than doing the right thing. Shame on them all.

CHAPTER NINETEEN

IN LOVE WITH LOVE

RUMORS WERE FLYING THAT ABC AND PARAMOUNT were talking about re-doing Love American Style but this time as a daytime strip-series. That meant five original half hour comedies a week. No one had ever attempted that before. Was it even possible? A big problem was that it would be very expensive to produce cer- tainly more than a game show or soap opera. ABC which was last in the ratings decided to bite the bullet. They hired Gordon Farr as Executive Producer mainly because he was coming off "Love Boat". The series are similar in the way they use guest stars in vignettes not related to each other. The first thing Gordy did besides pouring himself a large scotch was hire me as Su- pervising Producer. It was a no-brainer for him. He knew that most of his time would be taken up dealing with the network ex- ecutives and handling all the editing of the shows. The idea was to produce two stories per episode. That meant he would have to edit five shows a week involving ten stories. He knew he needed an organized person to select the stories go together which would be more complicated than planning D-Day. The or- der from ABC was a hundred shows in twenty weeks. I had the reputation as a 'horse', meaning I worked very hard and never seemed to tire and was a glutton for impossible situations. He wanted me to take charge of all scripts and re-writes. One hun- dred shows meant two-hundred stories to be written. We didn't know if it could be accomplished but I had hired a really good writing staff and was determined to make it work. Gordon and I would share the casting duties. Imagine how many actors we would need for two-hundred different stories. "Love" became the most popular program with SAG members.

We also realized that we couldn't bring in different directors for every story. It would take too long to get them up to speed so we hired two directors to do all the episodes. They would do alternate stories – it's called 'piggy-backing'. I hired David Yarnell as our line producer to handle the shooting schedule and budget. Opening titles had to be designed, sets built as soon as scripts were put into work and costumes designed once we knew what the stories were. It was the most exciting things I had ever done in my life. I never slept and spent almost every weekend in the office. Loved it. Paramount went to the various Guilds and got relief on payments because we were attempting a unique kind of series. We paid one thousand dollars per story, which was less than the WGA minimum but put a lot of free-lance writers to work. The Actor's union did the same thing because we were going to hire an inordinate number of actors. Their cooperation was es- sential to get the series done. I insisted that Paramount put ads in newspapers around the country advertising for stories. We didn't care whether the person sending the story in had any ex- perience or not. We were dealing in volume. The staff would quickly re-write anything coming in. I insisted that those outside 'writers' get an on-air credit as well as the thousand bucks. You can imagine the thrill I had calling a housewife in Nebraska and telling her that one of her stories was going to be on Love American Style. What a fun high. As a matter of fact, I bought a couple of stories from a young guy in Toronto. Years later he went on to produce "Cheers".

In order to keep all the departments flowing, Yarnell, held a production meeting every second week so that I could inform them what stories were coming up and what sets, props and wardrobe would be needed. ABC dedicated their largest tape stage to the program. We had sets for two or three shows in there at all times. As soon as we finished taping a story the set would be removed and a new one rolled in. It was an assembly line operation. The same thing held for costumes. There would be wardrobe for three or four stories on racks waiting for me to okay them. I'm exhausted just thinking about it.

This is an example of a typical day on Love American Style. I'd arrive at the studio around 7A.M. and check on the sets and props...making sure everything was in order. I'd then up to wardrobe and select the clothes for the stories to be taped that day. I'd walk to the office and make coffee. The staff usually came in around 8 or 8:30. I dug getting to the office early 'cause it was quiet and could take care of anything on my desk from the day before. I'd select a few writers to come down to a 'reading' of one of the stories we were going to rehearse. The other staff would continue writing whatever scripts they were working on. The ac- tors and director arrived around 9A.M. We'd begin the reading. Most of the stories ran about ten to twelve minutes. That way we could fit two stories in each episode. At the end of the reading we would go upstairs and start a re-write. The actors would begin rehearsing. New pages would be sent down to the stage and around noon we'd do a quick run-through. The actors would then go up to wardrobe, get fitted while we took another pass at the story. The final script would be sent to the actors at home. After lunch the process would begin again with a different director and different cast of actors. Each story got 2 re-writes in one day. Those two sets of actors would come in the next day and begin taping the stories. While these rehearsals and re-writes were go- ing on, we'd be taping two stories on our sets.

When we finished the hundred shows we all took deep breaths and a few bows from the network and studio. They said it couldn't be done – but we did it and did it well. As predicted the costs of production made it impractical for ABC to continue with it. Gordon and I were exhausted but proud as hell at our accom- plishment. It was the most stimulating professional experience I had ever had – keeping all those ball balls juggling in the air and not dropping one. I didn't want to think about what was next up for me – at least not for a few weeks.

CHAPTER TWENTY

THIS AND THAT AND MORE OF THAT

THE NEXT FEW YEARS SAW ME REVERT BACK TO MY gypsy way. I went from job to job seemingly treading water. I wasn't really ac- complishing much – having some laughs and working with friends but going nowhere fast. I'm not proud of any of the series I worked on with the exception of "HIS & HERS" a pilot I created.

"WEBSTER."

Was created by Stu Silver for Paramount and ABC in 1982. Stu's a really funny guy but totally neurotic. He became so pan-icked when he sold the show to the network that he refused to do it unless Bill D'Angelo became co-executive producer on it. He trusted and needed Bill's firm hand. In fact, he generously gave Bill a hefty piece of his ownership in Webster. The series went on the air starring Susan Clark, Alex Karras and introducing Emmanuel Lewis as Webster. Manny Lewis was less than 4-feet high and was almost a teenager when the series sold. He was adorable but untrained as an actor. He had made a name for himself doing a hamburger commercial. Paramount named Bruce Johnson as producer and two young writers from New York – Steve and Maddy Sunshine as story editors. Even though I didn't join Webster until the following year, the ugly stories about the series were legend. Susan Clark was the coldest woman any of us had ever met. Karras had been a professional football player for the Detroit Lions who had made a name for himself for being 'funny' on talk shows. Alex could act his way out of a paper bag, but no one told him that. He actually thought he was a clas- sical actor. Soon after playing "Mongo" in "BLAZING SADDLES" he had the chutzpah to tell a group of fellow actors that he "thought Larry Oliver was over-rated." The moron called Sir Law- rence, 'Larry'. I guess Alex played too many games without a helmet on. Alex and Susan were a frightening couple who didn't seem to like each other very much. The first time I met him he proudly said, "I haven't slept with my wife in years," Except he didn't say "slept". Manny Lewis was thrown together with these monsters and if it wasn't for Bill D'Angelo protecting him they would have eaten Manny alive. If you're unlucky enough to re- member the show Karras played a former football player whose best friend and teammate died leaving 'George' the responsibility of taking care of his son, Webster. Alex and Susan played newly- weds living in Chicago. In the pilot they decided to adopt this little black boy. Not a bad premise. Schmaltzy, but cute. Problems started on the show immediately. Susan Clark refused to allow the Webster character to call her mother or mom. She insisted that Manny call her 'Ma'am.' Real motherly, Susan, baby. She also never hugged Webster during the entire run of the series. She just played her character without any warmth. That worked out because Susan is devoid of warmth. Alex stayed out of the way in his dressing room smoking 'funny' cigarettes. Manny Lewis quietly stole the show from these two crazies.

Any new series has problems getting off the ground, but Webster turned it into an art form. Stu Silver decided that he wanted to write movies and basically disappeared leaving the show totally in the hands of Bill D'Angelo. No problem. If Bill could tame "Batman & Robin" which he did for a few years, he could certainly handle Susan and Alex, right? Wrong. He fought constantly with them trying to get them to act like professionals while looking to protect Manny. The series was an instant ratings hit because America fell in love with the little guy. With Stu Silver gone Bill gave the Sunshine's more and more authority. They became co-producers without the tile. When the season ended it became obvious that Susan and Alex didn't want Bill around an- ymore because he wouldn't take their crap. Goodbye Bill. The studio folded and removed him from the show allowing the Sun- shines to take over for him. They were now in charge of a net- work hit even though they had been in network television about three minutes. They had enormous egos and felt they deserved it. I was hired as Producer at the start of the second season for thirteen weeks to see how we'd get along. We didn't. At the end of thirteen weeks I happily went on my way.

"WE GOT IT MADE."

Was created by Gordon and Lynne Farr for MGM and Fred Silverman Productions in 1983. Jesus, getting rid of Silverman is tougher than getting rid of coronavirus! When Fred got fired from NBC there were no other networks for him to ruin so he became an independent producer. Brandon Tartikoff, now running NBC wanted to help out his old boss so he gave him several commitments. At an NBC meeting with the Farr's the network made it clear that they wanted to put on a 'rip-off' of THREE'S COMPANY. NBC need a young, sexy show. "We Got It Made" was the story of two young bachelors who advertise for a maid and this gorgeous 'Baywatch' type babe answered the ad. They hire her as a live-in. As a favor I helped Gordy and Lynne with writing the pilot and after it was done Gordon announced to the network that without my help the pilot never would have been done. It was nice of him, but honestly I was surprised that the series sold.

They hired Chick Mitchell and Geoff Neigher as Supervising producers and instead of making me producer they offered me a phony "Executive" title. Gordy blamed Lynne for the slight. Rather than make waves with 'friends' I accepted the demotion. I was very hurt but once again didn't have the guts to tell him to stick it and make waves with a friend. The cast was young, ener- getic and cute but the basic idea was pretty trite. The critics had a field day when the show went on the air basically saying it was a piece of shit. Alan Rafkin directed the series until he couldn't take the scorn from his fellow directors and quit. During produc- tion, after a run-through with NBC in which they gave their crea- tive notes and Silverman began to rant and rave. "Those god- damn network assholes have no right to tell us how to do our show." He went on and on about their interference. I yelled at him, "INTERFERENCE? You were the one who was responsible for network screwing with the producers and their series. It was you who had started the fucking thing in the first place!" Fred looked at me like I had a third eye. He forgot that he had started the disgusting process at CBS. We struggled along trying to produce the best series we could but nothing worked. The show was cancelled. Somewhere along the line I had gone to CBS and sold them my on pilot called "HIS & HERS". I'm still proud of that baby.

"HIS & HERS."

...was the story of a confirmed bachelor who against his better judgment falls in love and marries a woman with two teen- age daughters. This guy who was a man's man found himself suddenly surrounded by women when they move into his large, rent-controlled apartment. CBS like my script a lot and ordered a pilot. It was quite unusual for a free-lance writer to get a network commitment without a studio involved. I was thrilled beyond my belief. Maybe this was my chance to get out of this cycle of taking any job offered by creating my own series. I immediately in- formed Bernie Brillstein and his associate Sandy Wernick. I told them to try and get me a development deal someplace for really good money, because I would be bringing a pilot commitment with me. I waited and waited and finally Wernick called back when Chick and Geoff were in my office. I put him on 'speaker phone' without him knowing it. In his own obnoxious way Sandy announced,

"Kane we can't lay it off. No one wants to work with you. You're old hat." I couldn't believe my ears and Chick and Geoff shook their heads in astonishment that my manager would be crude enough to say something so hurtful to me. Sandy had the subtlety of a nuclear bomb. "If you're lucky we might be able to lay it off with Telepictures, but they ain't gonna pay you much money." Let's stop for a moment. I had a network deal for a pilot which might go to series...that ain't chopped liver! Writer/Producers work their whole lives to be in this situation. What the hell was going on? I asked him who the hell Telepictures was? He explained they were a syndication company looking to break into network programming.

They had just hired Frank Koenigsberg to head up their development company. I knew Frank when he was an agent at ICM. Sandy then told me to make up my mind – that it was Telepictures or nothing. When I hung up, Chick and Geoff began to laugh hysterically about 'the wonderful support I was getting from my managers." Talk about raining on my parade? Instead of cel- ebrating the Brillstein group made me feel like a poor relative asking for a handout. I'll be you're wondering why I didn't fire Brillstein on the spot and get other representation? I should have but I knew Bernie forever and we 'were friends' and I felt a certain loyalty. Okay, everyone together ---"SCHMUCK!!!!!!" I found out soon enough why Brillstein hadn't taken part in the discussion and why he suddenly was uninvolved with his old buddy's good fortune. I accepted the Telepictures deal. Again together – "SCHMUCK!!!!"

I hired a production staff and while sets were being built I began the all-important casting process. I wanted the pilot to have a certain look...not the typical TV tape set. The apartment was a large West Side pad. It was 'woodsy' with a fireplace and my designer did a marvelous job with it. It 'smelled' West End Avenue. Casting a pilot is always a difficult assignment. All the networks order their pilots at the same time so everyone is scrambling for the same acceptable actors. The networks have to approve the stars so they have their "A" list. Unless you get lucky early on your choices are soon people on the "B" list or "C" list which doesn't bode well for the pilot's being picked up. I wanted a very masculine, macho type actor in the male lead. I had some choices in mind but between Koenigsberg and CBS we had a difficult time agreeing on anybody. The truth is a pow- erful production company always had first crack at the best ac- tors but no one had ever heard of Telepictures so we were going to suck hind tit. You don't get many opportunities to do a pilot so I wasn't going to be railroaded into a choice. Brillstein didn't do shit to help in the process. One day I got a nervous call from Jean Guest, the head of casting for CBS. Jean told me that I had to hire Nick Apollo Forte who Woody Allen had just used in his movie "Broadway Danny Rose".

When I asked why all the heat on this guy, she explained that all three networks where in a bidding war to make a deal with Forte. I had seen the movie and loved it but didn't think Nick was right for my lead, however, I agreed to meet with him. CBS had hidden Nick and his family away in a cabin at the Beverly Hills Hotel. Koenigsberg's attitude was if CBS wanted him that was all that mattered. A typical reaction from an agent. Nick came into my office the next day and we talked for a while. He admitted that he didn't understand all the publicity and hype he was getting. The truth is he wasn't an actor at all but a fisherman from Long

Island in New York. That's how he made a living for his wife and eight kids. He also used to sing at weddings, bar-mitzvahs, parties, etc. He told me how Woody Allen found him a couple years before on a visit to NYC. Nick had put a couple of his homemade records in some record stores. He would sneak them into "Italian Music" folders when no one was looking. He figured that maybe somebody would fine them and book him for their next Anniversary or cocker spaniel's birthday. Nick was being totally honest with me. When Woody was casting Danny Rose he sent his casting executive out to pick up some Italians records so he could get a feeling for the kind of music he wanted to use in the film. This woman walked into one of the record stores that Forte had planted his records, picked one up and brought it back to Woody. Talk about a longshot! This reads like a bad "B" movie but is the truth. Nick Forte had a big picture of himself on the record cover. Allen took one look at his face and told his casting person to fine Nick Apollo Forte. She couldn't track him down. None of the theatrical unions had him listed. Finally they were able to locate him through the musician's union. Woody called but Nick was out on his fishing boat. When Nick got home his kids excitedly told him Woody Allen had called and wanted Nick to call him back. Nick had never heard of Woody Allen. His kids explained who he was and Nick called Woody back. Allen asked Nick if he could come to NYC and meet him and Forte agreed and when they met, Woody kept looking at him and finally asked Nick to read some scenes with him. They did and Woody hired this professional fisherman to star in the movie. Great story, right? Trouble was that Nick Apollo Forte couldn't act. They shot the movie one line at a time according to Nick. It was put together in the editing room.

Nick who was totally honest was happily telling me this un-believable story. I thanked him for coming in, wished him luck and soon he was out the door. I called Jean Guest and told her I wasn't even going to consider Forte for my pilot. She was a little pissed off and hired him for another CBS pilot. The poor guy was fired in two days when it became apparent that he knew nothing about acting. Rather than embarrass himself anymore he agreed to go back to Long Island and resume his fishing career. Thinking back on this story makes me think of the phrase, "The inmates are running the asylum." I still can't believe that it really hap- pened. Back to reality. A lot of time was wasted and casting was getting even more urgent. Casting the female lead was easy. Everyone loved Shelly Fabares. Shelly was attractive, bright, had strength and knows her business. It was late so casting the male lead really became a huge problem. All the "A" and "B" listed ac- tors had been hired already. I settled on Richard Kline from "Three's Company." Richard played the next-door neighbor on the series and was good at it. Some actors are great next-door neigh-bors' but aren't really "leads." Richard is a nice guy and in- telligent but frankly didn't have the 'balls' I was looking for. I hired him.

The other characters in the pilot were great and I couldn't have been happier. As the youngest daughter I cast a relative newcomer named Shannon Doherty. If I knew she was going to grow up and be so sexy I would have married her. Our director was a young guy named Sam Weisman who went on to win Emmy's on Family Ties. Rehearsals went along very well. I had the occasional run-in with Koenigsberg who had never been involved with a comedy before. The bosses of Telepictures were absolutely thrilled and promised that they would never forget me for getting them started in network television. They were men of their word which is pretty rare in the entertainment industry. We taped the pilot and it went really well. Telepictures seemed happy and so did CBS, I began editing the pilot and wanted to do some- thing very unusual for a comedy tape show. I wanted to score the complete half hour like Woody Allen did in "Manhattan". Since I had written a love story I wanted romantic music throughout. Frank K. objected (what a fucking surprise) and we really battled over the music. We finally compromised and I was able to put in more romantic music than normal. I turned the pilot in and alt- hough we had high hopes for it..."HIS & HERS" didn't make the fall schedule.

I found out why Bernie Brillstein had made himself scarce on this project. I was going over the budget with my line producer and found an interesting item buried on one of the pages. As my manager Bernie was taking 10% of my fee as writer/producer of "HIS & HERS". He deserved that. But, I suddenly discov- ered that Brillstein was also getting a package commission from Telepictures. That's a no-no. He was double-dipping. If he was getting a package commission it was illegal for him to take ten percent of my fee. What he was doing was illegal and had I blown the whistle on him he would have been in deep trouble. He soon became a large stockholder in Telepictures. It became obvious why Bernie and Sandy Wernick placed my pilot with them. "No one wants your pilot except Telepictures" became crystal clear. I had gotten screwed by my representatives. CBS was so pleased with the job I had done that they gave me an open pilot commit- ment by way of thanks. Many months later, Telepictures bought a controlling interest in Lorimar Productions. Lorimar was a very successful production company headquartered at the old

MGM studios. Now don't yell at me, okay? I called Brillstein, who after my pilot seemed strangely distant – probably feeling guilty – if pricks like him ever feel guilty – and reminded him that Telepictures had said that they wanted to keep working with me. He arranged a meeting with David Saltzman – who had taken over as Lorimar President. At our meeting David talked about the possibility of making me his assistant and heading the television development department. I was thrilled with the possibility. He said if that didn't work out I would given would be given a development deal at Lorimar. Telepictures hadn't forgotten what I had done for them. David was going on a month's long vacation and wanted to think about both possibilities. The month seemed like two years to me. When he returned I called Brillstein and told him to get Saltzman on the phone and find out what he had decided. Bernie got back to me in a few days and 'claimed' there was nothing for me at Lorimar. I knew this was total bullshit and that the 'momser' was up to one of his games. I won't bore you with the details or why this sick fuck was doing what he was doing. I talked to Saltzman myself and got a development deal and his company. A deal was made and I moved into my offices on the MGM lot. At the same time Mr. Brillstein became President of Lorimar Pictures. I know it's about time but I FIRED Bernie as my manager. I know IT WAS ABOUT TIME!

Before I put the Bernie Brillstein story to bed – the last time he and I spent any time together was at a breakfast at the Polo Lounge of the Beverly Hills Hotel. He started complaining about Gordon Farr not wanting to pay him a commission on some deal. He ranted that Gordy was disloyal and that's why he loved me. I was always there for him and everyone else. Whenever he called me for a favor for one of his clients I always came through. That he would never forget how I let him stay at my house during his divorce from Laura. He told me that I was a good friend. He even sort of apologized for seeming distant lately but he had been working hard and the death of John Belushi had really rocked him. Suddenly, I'm goddamn Mother Teresa to him and he forgot about all the shit he had been putting me through. I realized that Brillstein wasn't of sound mind and was glad to finally be ride of the asshole. Should have done it years ago.

CHAPTER TWENTY-ONE
CANADA O'CANADA

BILL D'ANGELO HAD BECOME PRESIDENT OF GROSSO-Jacobson Productions. Sonny Grosso was a legendary New York detective and was one of the guys who broke the famous French Connec- tion drug case. When Sonny retired he and Larry Jacobson formed a production company in NYC. They had done many MOW's about police cases and had finally branched into series television. They hired Bill D'Angelo to head up their production company because of his vast network experience. They were producing a late-nite CBS cop series "Night Heat" which was being filmed in Toronto. They had just sold their second series to CBS "Diamonds" which was also going to be shot in Toronto. Bill flew up there to get the new series started. He hated cold weather with a passion. After a few months in Toronto he realized winter would be arriving and that his toes would freeze. He wanted out.

He talked Sonny and Larry into bringing me up to run Diamonds. I packed my long underwear and flew up there. Toronto is one of the most civilized cities in the world. I fell in love with the place. It was beautiful, charming, clean and safe. The people are wonderfully friendly and its cultural life is second only to New York. I got a new job, new adventure and new country. What could be better?

Bill was living at the Four Seasons Hotel in Yorkville sec- tion of the city. Yorkville is the 5th Avenue or Rodeo Drive of To- ronto. It has great shopping, restaurants and beautiful women. I flew up and checked into the hotel and remained there for three months. Bill had a large suite on the same floor as my room which we used as an office on weekends. D'Angelo never left the hotel unless it was to go to our production office or a location that we were filming. I called Bill "Nero" because he conducted himself in a superior and royal manner. He just expected things to be done for him and besides "Nero" I took to calling him "Godfather". He liked his comfort and liked room-service even more. He figured that if Sonny and Larry didn't bitch then why not pamper your- self? When he left to finally left to fly back to L.A. after six months at the 4 Seasons he had run up a bill of almost eighty-eight thou- sand dollars. The hotel should have put up a bronze plaque on the door of his suite. On weekends, I would try to talk Bill into going out and investigating the city. He refused. It was getting too cold and he didn't wear socks so the hell with sight-seeing. If he wouldn't walk, I offered to carry him on my back. "Nero" just shook his head, "No" and gave me the royal wave.

I told this story at my darling friend Bill's funeral in 2002. He and I would have breakfast together every morning at the 4 Seasons and the head for the office. After a full day of filming we would return to the hotel and order from room service. The hotel staff saw us together all the time – morning and night – and finally assumed that we were gay lovers. They began turning down his bed on both sides and leave little chocolate mints on both pillows. What a hoot. The real reason I didn't say anything to the cham- bermaids was I really loved those chocolates.

Around Christmas we both flew back to the U.S. for the holidays and Brill remained. I flew back to Toronto and took over the show. Sonny and Larry weren't about to keep paying for my hotel room so they got me an apartment overlooking Lake On- tario. It was a gorgeous sight to wake up each winter morning and look out at frozen Lake Ontario. I stayed in Toronto almost eight months and loved every bit of it. The best things about working on location, is that you live on your per-diem and bank your salary. They paid for my apartment and were given a car to use and expenses so it's a heckuva way to get financially healthy. "Diamonds" was a one-hour private-eye show. I had never done an hour action series before and I learned a great deal doing one. It was also nice not having to worry about writing 4 jokes per page. The concept of the series was that this ex- husband and wife team who had been actors on a private-eye TV series, which had been cancelled, decided to become real PIs and open their own agency. His cousin was a real police Lieutenant who could throw business their way. It was a nice commercial idea with lots of opportunity for humor as well as ac- tion. Since the series was airing on CBS in the U.S. and a Cana- dian network the show was set in a generic city someplace in the northern hemisphere. There were no identifying signs on police cars or uniforms.

My job until Bill left was to work on the set with the actors, fixing any script problems as well as seeing that things ran smoothly during shooting. Because Bill and I were Americans we had no titles – the Canadian government gives producers money not only to encourage Canadian productions, but to see that Ca- nadian personnel are used on various shows. Everyone knew that D'Angelo was in charge of Diamonds and that I was going to take over...we just couldn't have our names appear on the screen. Who cared? The cast was made up of Canadian actors with the exception of the female lead who was American. Some- how they got her 'grandfathered' in. The directors, crews and writers were all Canadians and the talent pool was fabulous. There were hundreds of 'classically' trained Canadian actors just waiting for the opportunity to work. The directors were excellent and worked very hard to keep on schedule. When I returned to Toronto a few years later to do a comedy series I found a dearth of comedy direc- tors and writers. The good, ones had all moved to the States. The crews on the set were hard working and never complained. Their work ethic could be topped.

Our lead actor Nick Campbell could be a problem. He was either very good, or if he was sniffing 'white powder' became crazy as a loon. Nick came from a long line of wonderful Cana- dian actors and it was sad that he wouldn't take responsibility for his actions. I understand that he has cleaned up his act and is still not only working as an actor but had become a very fine director. The same problem was true with the actor playing his cousin. He had been fired from "Saturday Night Live" for bad be- havior and it followed him to 'Diamonds.' When Nick and Tony were on drugs, they caused nothing but problems and delays. It had gotten so bad that the American actress would 'toot' up just not to feel left out. Everybody in Toronto knew about the drug use on our set but Sonny Grosso refused to play the 'bad cop'. (note: Tony finally was committed to a mental hospital because of his drug habit.)

I began to spend all my time, on the set, putting out fires and arguing with the damn actors. The more drugs they used the more irrational their behavior. Besides acting like a kindergarten teacher I still had to supervise the scripts, pick locations and help cast the show. In spite of all this grief the show was a good one. No one could really put an end to all the bullshit going on except Sonny Grosso. He was afraid of losing his temper and beating the shit out of the actors so he just ignored it all. Sonny spent all his time editing the shows and when he would complain to me that the actors weren't saying 'their lines' I'd point out that I could only fight with them so long that we had to get the work out some- how. If he gave me the authority to 'fire' someone the actors knew I could bitch all I wanted but they weren't in danger. When Sonny kept his temper in check the problems remained mine. After twenty-six shows CBS changed their late-night program- ming and decided that cop shows had to go. USA Network quickly picked up "Diamonds" for the next season. Frankly, I was beaten down by the constant arguing with the three leads and the lack of support from Grosso. I came up with what I thought was a great solution for us: I wrote a script in which the police Lieutenant was shot and killed. I knew that if Sonny allowed us to shoot that script the other actors would get the message and straighten up. Everyone else on the production staff told Grosso that we had to shoot the script. He thought about it and in the end begged me to re-write the script and let "Tony" live. I told Sonny that it was his series but that I couldn't come back for another season. It was just to frustrating for me and not worth my time and health. I left Toronto in May and knew one day I would return. I made too many good friends and enjoyed the city too much not to return.

On my first weekend back in Los Angeles I was walking around Century City people watching and shopping. Suddenly I heard a voice say, "Arnie, when did you get back in town?" I turned at it was fat Bernie Brillstein and his two little sons. I hadn't thought of him in years. He gave me a big hug and made like we were still friends. I wanted to puke. Was it possible that he didn't realize how much he hurt me and many of his other clients? All of us had been shocked by his abandoning us as if we never existed. Trust me I didn't need that casual meeting in Century City. It got me thinking and getting furious all over again. I had to get my angst off my chest to let him know how I felt. I intended to write him a long, scathing letter basically telling him what a duplicitous bastard he was. Bill D'Angelo told me that I should call Brillstein's office and insist on a face to face meeting...that I should confront him in person. I took his advice and called asking for a meeting which was arranged for the following week. Man, I prepared what I was going to say and couldn't wait. I wanted to blow that fat fuck out of his chair. When I went into his office and began to give him a piece of my mind – he interrupted me. He said he knew I was pissed off at him but that he didn't care. He had made a conscious decision that he was only going to worry about his own career and that if it hurt friends and clients – so be it! He knew he was totally wrapped up in himself but that's the way it was. The only person he cared for was Bernie Brillstein. When he was finished there was nothing for me to say. The prick admitted everything I was going to accuse him of – so I turned a left. Talk about a bummer.....

Things were really slow after "Diamonds" and I decided that I couldn't afford to keep my Hollywood Hills home and my condo in Palm Springs. I decided to sell the Hollywood Hills home because of the peacefulness and joy I experienced in Palm Springs was more important than anything. I sold the house even though I had many, many fond memories of the nights I spent in it and the women I spent them with.

Financially, I was in big trouble. My parents were draining any savings I had. They began to get frail and their medical bills were mounting up. I, also, had to buy them a new car and move them into a new condo in West Palm Beach, Florida. I thought my problems were going to be solved when I read that Gordon Farr sold "We Got It Made" for syndication. I expected him to hire me but he didn't. I was stunned. We met for a drink and I was telling him how desperate things were getting – and something I never did before I began crying. We were sitting in this Mexican restaurant and tears were rolling down my cheeks. I had lost con- trol and was cracking up. Gordy just stared at me not offering to help in any way. I went home depressed and defeated. My ex- partner and friend wasn't there for me. That incident was an eye- opener. I should have realized it before, but I now knew that I couldn't expect people to give a shit about my problems or feel- ings. The only person I could count on was myself. It was time to grow up and take my life in my own hands. Just because I'm a nice guy doesn't mean I was owed anything by anybody. Did this knowl- edge change my life? Keep reading.

One day Sam Denoff and I were sitting around when I told him about an idea I had for a comedy series. I wanted to do a male version of "Golden Girls". It would be a chauvinistic and funny male show. It would deal with a group of guys who get together each week to play poker, but the 'real' reason was to bond and complain about their lives, work, wives, children and girlfriends. We called it "THE GAME." We went to see Normal Powell who was head of in- house CBS Productions. Norman loved the idea and ordered a script from us. No one had ever done a totally male series before. We had a ball writing it be- cause Sam and I are basically chauvinistic pigs and we just let it all hang out. While we were working on it, Barbara Corday, had left Columbia tele-vision and was appointed second in command a CBS under Kim LeMasters. We couldn't have been happier. Barbara worked for us on Turnabout and was a friend as was Kim. We handed in our first draft to Norman and his female as- sistant. We were a little nervous that she might find it too rough on women but she loved the script. Norman told us he was rec- ommending that CBS shoot the pilot immediately. "The Game" was the funniest script he had read in years. Norman confidently sent the script to Corday to get her approval. Sam and I, in the meantime, were getting great feedback from others at CBS who hadn't read it, but had heard how funny it was. We figured we were golden especially with our friend Barbara reading it. What we hadn't factored in was that now that Corday was not just an executive – but had become an angry, feminist woman who had lost her funny bone. Her husband Barney had divorced her and married Sharon Gless and that had obviously changed her.

When Barbara read the script she SCREAMED that something as 'disgusting' and 'chauvinistic' as "The Game" would never be on any network she had anything to do with. She drew a line in the sand and insisted that if our script was shot she would leave the network. How nuts is that? Suddenly CBS was making decisions not based on quality but their acceptability to fringe groups. Kim LeMasters refused to intervene on our behalf. He didn't want to get into a beef With Corday so soon after she arrived. He didn't wait a little longer before he destroyed her ca- reer at CBS. Sam and I were unhappy that "The Game" didn't go on the air but we were really proud of that script. It was bitching funny.

I was offered a job to go back to Toronto to produce a Canadian series which had been bought by the USA Network. I had a breakfast meeting with Richard Borchiver of Paragon Enter- tain- ment, the Canadian company, and the USA people. They had sent me the pilot of the show which was lousy. I told them the original concept should be scrapped and that we should make it a half hour comedy about a mother, two children and their "talk- ing dog" which was the trick of the series. It was a "Mr. Ed" with a Saint Bernard". USA loved my idea which made Borchiver very happy. Paragon had never done a TV series before so USA made it clear that I was totally in charge. I was the creative per- son and should be allowed to do my thing. I knew from my last trip to Toronto that comedy writers and directors were very scarce in Toronto and that I would have to put a staff together in L .A. The first person I called was Bruce Johnson. He hadn't hooked up with a series yet so I begged him to join me in Toronto. When I explained the financial benefits of doing a series up there he agreed to do it. He and I hired two young women who were coming off a season as writers on "Full House." Julie Strassman and Shari Scharfer were bright, young and full of enthusiasm. They were excited about working in Toronto and maybe meeting some illegible Canadian bachelors. I figured we could probably hire a couple of young comedy writers up there and teach them what we needed. Before Bruce and I flew up for a survey trip we hired to Canadian comedy directors for the series: Perry Rose- mont and Stuart Gillard. We knew them and thought we were in good hands with them directing. We were in pretty good shape staff-wise and we got on our plane.

CHAPTER TWENTY-TWO
DOGHOUSE

WHILE WE WERE IN TORONTO WE ARRANGED FOR office space and began hiring office staff. Richard Borchiver took us to lunch to meet the actress who played the mother in the series. SHELLY PETERSON was a fairy well-known actress who happened to be married to David Peterson, the Premier of Ontario. David was predicted to become the next Prime Minister of Canada. He was the JFK of that Country...young, classy and handsome. Shelley was a doll and Bruce and I were pleased that we had at least one real actor on the series. James Wolvett who played the oldest son went on the co-star with Clint Eastwood in the "Unforgiven". The two kids playing the other children had no experience at all. After we got things settled in Toronto, including apartments for all of us overlooking Lake Ontario, we headed back to Los Ange- les. I decided to create a strong comedy part for an actor who had worked for me in 'Diamonds', named Barry Flatman. If Barry lived in the U.S. he'd have starred in his own series. He was bril- liantly funny. We made him the next-door neighbor who was a local TV weatherman. Think: Ted Knight on Mary Tyler Moore. I still laugh at some of Barry's appear- ances. We wrote three scripts in Los Angeles and gave out assign- ments to some Cana- dian writers who were living in the States. I always liked to go into a series with as many scripts completed as possible before filming begins. Bruce and I flew back to Toronto and began seri- ous pre- production. "DOG HOUSE" was airing on YTV, the lead- ing children's network and we had meetings with them just to let them know we knew what we were doing. Everyone was helpful and positive. Bruce knew our dog trainers from Hollywood. Roger and Matilda flew up with BODIE, the sweet St. Bernard. They were the best animal trainers I had ever seen and BODIE, named "Digby" in the series never disappointed us. The trick, of course, was how to get Digby to talk. They experi- mented with peanut butter, chew sticks and finally settle on a beef jerky type stick which Digby would chew on...stimulating speech. The idea was to 'lay-in' a human voice when we mixed the show. Julie and Shari arrived and were driven to their apartments on Lakeshore Drive. The apartments were furnished beautifully, but a little problem crept up that we hadn't anticipated. Julie Strassman was afraid of heights and her pad was on the 24th floor overlook- ing the Lake. Julie would literally crawl on her hands and knees to open and close her drapes – petrified to look out. When she en- tertained company she would crawl around on all fours serv- ing drinks and hors d'oeuvers. Who said comedy writers were nor- mal?

We started auditioning 'voice-over' performers looking for someone to do "Digby's" voice. No one seemed right. USA was heavily involved in that search. I figured we'd find the right voice eventually, but we needed to start production. Digby's 'voice would be needed for several weeks until we got into post-pro-duc- tion. I, also, hired a Canadian writer named Rick Adamson, whose spec script I read and liked. It was a chance to train a new writer and give him experience on a series. Bruce, Julie, Shari and I hung out together and all fell in love with Toronto. The girls met some guys and Bruce and I would get reports every morning about their escapades with Toronto's bachelors. The girls were lucky the vice squad didn't deport them. I'm kidding but Julie eventually married a young lawyer she met that year. They adopted a young child but sadly the marriage went down the tubes.

We finally began filming "DOG HOUSE". Our scripts were read on Monday mornings. USA would fly up an executive to be there for the reading as would YTV. They'd give us some notes and then we'd go back to our offices to re- write the script. Since the show was shot single-camera – like feature film – most TV comedies use multi-cameras but because we were working with a dog we couldn't do that. During our Monday readings Bruce Johnson would 'read' Digby's lines and break all of us up and I finally decided why not have Bruce do that job on the series? So, he became the 'voice' of Digby and earned extra money for doing it. Everyone seemed pleased with our shows. Soon after we be-gan production David Peterson decided to call for an early elec-tion in Ontario. Everyone predicted he would be a shoo-in to be reelected Premier. When Shelley wasn't needed on the set, she would make appearances and speeches for him like a political wife does in the States. David would visit "Dog House" occasionally with their three kids: Ben, Chloe and Adam. Since Shelley's shooting schedule was hectic, David, even though Premier of the largest Province in Canada became "Mr. Mom." He would take the kids to school every day and pick them up. Canada seems to have its priorities right. Family is more important than any political office. Peterson used to travel with just a driver – no bodyguards, no undercover cops, no press secretary – it blew me away. When his official duties were over for the day, David, like to wear jeans or a sweat suit around town. Sadly, Peterson was given bad po- litical advice – the conservative movement in America its way up to Canada without the liberals realizing it. He was defeated badly much to the surprise of so-called political experts in Toronto. He got knocked on his ass. Shelley was obviously distraught but Da- vid took it with good humor. To me he looked like he had swal- lowed a cuff link. At dinner one night I asked him if he would con- sider acting on one of our shows for laughs. He happily agreed but only if he wasn't playing a politician. When I asked what he wanted to play, he said "somebody normal...like a janitor." So, David Peterson, still in office played a janitor in an episode of Dog House. The series got a lot of publicity about his acting gig. On the show we were filming at a middle-school early one morning. The deal was that we had to be done before classes began. We were shooting a scene in a school corridor with James Wolvett talking to the school janitor (David) when a couple of real teachers arrived early. They almost died when they saw Peterson in his janitor jump-suit mopping the floor. Those sweet women actually believed that because David had been defeated he'd taken a janitorial job to support his family. Bless them Ca- nadians will believe anything including that Spam is a food deli- cacy.

Another quirk of fate happened during "Dog House". I received a panic call from Gordon Farr in Los Angeles telling me that he was in financial problems and asking for my help. I kid you not! Instead of reminding him that when I was in trouble and asked for his help he didn't raised a finger for me, I decided to do what I could to for him. Since Gordy was a Canadian, I could use him to write scripts for the show. I guaranteed him ten scripts which meant over one-hundred thousand dollars to him. I just never learned!

All in all I spent about one year in Toronto on Dog House. We were hoping to be picked up for a second season but although USA really liked the series they decided to forego children's programming entirely. YTV couldn't afford to finance the series themselves so "Dog House" was 'put- down'. I really felt sad about leaving the city again. Part of me wanted to stay or at least come back soon. I didn't have to wait too long for that to become a reality.

CHAPTER TWENTY-THREE
THE BLACK DAYS

BUCKLE YOUR SEAT BELTS. WHAT FOLLOWS IS A BUMPY ride. The fun and games are over! When I arrived back in the States in 1991 I didn't know what to expect. I had been gone a year and things had really changed in television. It's difficult to believe, but in the space of that one year "ageism" which had always been a dirty little secret when hiring staffs had become a full-fledged ep- idemic...as network and studio honchos got younger and younger they didn't want to work with older writer and producers unless they were someone like Gary Marshall or Norman Lear...a person with a track record that they couldn't just ignore. They just felt more comfortable dealing with people their own age. Larry Gelbart who created "MASH" nicknamed them, "Fetuses in three-piece suits." People my age had become unemployable. We were euphemistically called "grays". These network 'mom- sers' didn't want 'grays' working on their network shows. The only true value in television was youth!

None of us should have been surprised. Advertisers had been spending billions for years trying to attract younger custom- ers. TV programming was geared toward the eighteen to thirty- five-year-old market. Movies were being released mainly for younger and younger audiences. America was focused on stay- ing young. Age discrimination was everywhere you looked. "Age- ism" is ILLEGAL, of course but it became the dirty-not-so-secret world in show business. The executives playing this dirty game never could sway out loud, "you're too old!" they were too smart for that. Without legal proof we couldn't sue the bastards.

The WGA tried to take networks, studios, production com- panies, agents and managers to court for years but had been unsuccessful. Suddenly none of us could get pitch meetings at networks. We were unable to be considered for jobs that we were doing for years. We had no value in the marketplace. Our talent and years of experience didn't count for anything. As a matter of fact it was used against us. Except for Bill D'Angelo who was still working for Grosso-Jacobson none of my other friends could get a job. We were all in the same boat and it was the Titanic! My worst fears had come true. All my adult life, I had believed my business success was the only measurement of my value as a person. If I wasn't working I was a non-person in my own eyes. I began to sink into a deep depression which got deeper and deeper as the year went along. I became terribly angry and un- happy with my life because my work had always been my salva- tion.

A few months into my funk, my Mother died in Florida. I flew down for the funeral, but honestly felt nothing. My Father was devastated having been married to her for 64 years. I went through the motions trying to support my father who quickly be- came a helpless old man. I arranged for him to move into a re- tirement home and paid one year in advance. I was the only one he could depend on. After I got back to Palm Springs my life con- sisted on playing golf, going to the gym, swimming and getting sun. Pretty nice, for someone retired, but pretty empty, for a guy who needed to work. In hindsight, what I needed was serious and intensive psychiatric help. Instead I began to booze a lot. I was living in denial hoping things would turn around business-wise. I dreamed it was a bad dream and that everyone (ME) would come to their senses and want to hire me again. I hid most of my de- pression from friends because I could always be funny and that covered up my feeling. It took about six months for me to finally admit that I wasn't living some dream, it was reality. That feeling of help-lessness and hopelessness was so overwhelming that I began to think about ending my life. (I told you at the start of this chapter that the fun and games were over.) I was getting increas- ingly angry and bitter and didn't like the person I was turning into. My constant complaining was beginning to bore the hell out of me. At the end of March 1992 I played in the Pro-Am of the Dinah Shore LPGA Tournament at Mission Hills Country Club. I knew most of the celebrities playing and enjoyed playing golf with the lady pros. When that was finished I decided to COMMIT SUI-CIDE. It was just a matter of picking the right moment. Now this is going to sound really crazy, but I began to look forward to it. Maybe I could no longer produce TV sitcoms but I sure as hell could produce my own suicide.

I approached it like a television series. I made sure that every-thing was in order – that there were no loose threads. My will and 'living will' were written. I called my Father and told him I was going to Europe on a job and wouldn't be able to be reached. If he needed anything he had instruction to call my business manager who would take care of it. I even told my friends at Mis- sion Hills that I was leaving on a long trip. Shit, I hadn't felt this good in over six months. I finally had control over something – my own death. Everything was covered. I was back in charge. It must sound really strange but all the activity leading up to my suicide gave me some focus. MY lifestyle had finally caught up with me. Afraid to allow women to get too close to me, left me without anyone I could lean on. My distrust and fear of being 'hurt' had come back to haunt me. Here I was in a big-time crises and I was alone. Sure, I had good friends but never allowed my- self to become weak in their eyes and my macho stupidity that a man never shows vulnera-bility helped lead me to where I was. I had had a nervous break-down when I was nine years old and was in and out of analyst's offices through the years but never serious about dealing with my depression. The chemical imbal- ance that I was diagnosed with in Toronto a year later would have made all the difference in the world to me. I have been on anti- depressives ever since. They have helped me become a new man. Just think, I truly believed that unless I was working at my craft that I had no justification for being. That Arnold Kane's whole existence and happiness was dependent on a job. If it wasn't so pathetic and insane it would be laughable. I wasn't laughing in 1992.

On the weekend of June 14th 1992 Bill D'Angelo took a condo near mine for his 60th birthday. All of his family came down to celebrate it. We were all cooking something special for the party and have a ball. Bill was flying to NYC on the 15th for a meeting with Grosso-Jacobson. I had decided that on the even- ing of the 14th I would take a bucket full of pills which I had been hoard- ing for months. During that weekend I wrote letter to my closest friends explaining why I felt I was doing the right thing and mailed it them during the weekend knowing they'd receive them after I had swallowed my pills. After the party I wished Bill a safe trip and told him that I loved him. He thought it strange but didn't say anything to me. I rarely told anyone that I loved them. I, of course, did but just had problems saying those words. The next morning, I went through my usual routine obviously not let- ting on what I intended to do that night. I had booked a room in a nearby hotel overlooking my beloved mountains to end my life. The last thing I wanted to see were those gorgeous mountains turning purple and pink.

Around 5pm I wrote a note explaining why I was committing suicide which intended to place near the empty bottles of pills. I closed up my condo, walked to the hotel went to my room and sat looking at the mountains. I swallowed the pills remembering that I felt very at peace and calm. I lay down on the bed and 'went to sleep'. I have never been a believer in fate or karma – or even tofu – for that matter. I'm probably too cynical for that. But, I ob- viously wasn't meant to succeed in my suicide attempt. Strange things began to happen that were unusual. On Tuesday morning Gordon Farr called my condo and got no answer. I had discon- nected my answering machine. For some strange reason he be- came very nervous about that. He kept calling and getting no an- swer. He then called Bill in New York and asked him if I had men- tioned going away during the weekend? Bill told Gordon about my saying that "I loved him". That was unlike something I would have normally said and they both got worried. Bill called the man- ager of my condo complex and asked him to check on me. Todd rang my doorbell and getting no response looked in my window but didn't see anything unusual and reported that back to D'An- gelo. Gordon in the meantime had called my friend Neil Sherman and asked if he had heard from me? Neil told him no but that I had seemed 'strange' last time we spoken. Gordon and Neil de- cided to drive down to Palm Springs and check on things. Bill told Sonny and Larry that he had to get back to Los Angeles, that something wasn't kosher. He was worried about me and caught the next plane back. It's still a little spooky that all these people were getting bad vibes at the same time.

While Gordy and Neil were driving down, Gordon's wife started calling hospital in Palm Springs thinking maybe I had had an accident. When the boys arrived at my condo they had Todd let them into my condo and they found some papers I had left including my will. They knew immediately what I had done and rushed out to go to the Police. As they jumped into Neil's car they heard an Ambulance siren nearby. They decided to check it out and arrived at the hotel at the same time as the Paramedics did. They arrived at my room at the same time as the police and med- ical people. They found me lying on the floor, still breathing, but barely. I was rushed to the hospital and wheeled into ER. The doctors didn't think I would pull through. Bill arrived Wednesday morning and since I had named him 'executor' of my living will he had to grapple with the possibility of pulling the plug if that became necessary.

A girlfriend had been called and they all sat around wondering what Act Two was going to be. Finally, on Wednesday night the doctors announced that I was going to live. Gordon and Neil went back to L.A. and Bill and the girl remained. Sometime on Thursday I opened my eyes and saw them standing around my bed. I couldn't speak because there were tubes down my throat connected to a ventilator which was helping me breathe. From what I remember I wasn't angry at failing at suicide but nei- ther do I remember being happy to be alive. All I know was that I was very sick and weak as a baby and couldn't even stand up by myself. I was suffering from pneumonia and the after-effects of the emergency staff's attempt to keep me alive. Doctors kept coming in and telling me that I was lucky to be alive. I'm not sure I agreed with them at the time. Before they would release me a hospital psychiatrist visited and asked why I had tried to kill my- self. I asked him how old he was and he told me 63. I asked how he would feel if he knew that he could never, ever work again just because he was 63? He admitted that he would be angry as hell and I smiled and said now you know how I felt. He asked if I thought I would attempt suicide again and I told him "No". That I had tried, it didn't work and now was time to move on with my 'new' life. I did agree, however, to get psychological help that I obviously needed. My pneumonia took quite a while to go away. I, also, could eat because the tubes had done big time damage to my throat. In fact I couldn't speak above a whisper for six months, dropped to 138 pounds and received some nerve dam- age in my right foot. The pain lasted almost a year. The conclu- sion: if you are going to try and commit suicide – do it success- fully. If you fuck up the results can be worse than the act itself.

Fortunately, I was told about a brilliant psychiatrist named Susan Young. With her help I began to look at the layers of bullshit that I had built around myself. My defenses were stronger than the Taliban. Susan wouldn't let me get away with any of my 'games' and insisted that I really work on my problems. We were making some great progress on my problems and we decided that it wasn't healthy for me to remain in my environment and that it might be better if I moved to Toronto and start over again. I applied for immigration papers and when they finally came through I flew up to Toronto to find a place to live. I found a fabulous duplex in Yorkville which was furnished beautifully and signed he rental papers. I flew back to Palm Springs knowing I had a great place to begin my new life. I decided to drive to Toronto. I was in no hurry.

Before we close this chapter I feel I should be totally honest about my attempted suicide. I wasn't embarrassed about trying it. At the time and in the state of mind I was in – it seemed logical and a solution to a depression that had taken over my life. I'm happy it wasn't successful – or this would be the last page of my memoir.

CHAPTER TWENTY-FOUR
STARTING OVER

ON JUNE 28, 1993 I ARRIVED IN CANADA AS A 'LANDED immi- grant' ready for a new start. My status as a 'landed immigrant' allowed me all the social services that any Canadian had includ- ing free medical, the only thing I could do was vote. Like that bumper sticker: "Today was the first day of the rest of my life." The drive across American was relaxed and enjoyable. For the first time in many years I didn't have an agenda. I was going to allow things to happen at their own pace. I promised myself that it was okay to take my time and get my footing in this new Country. I had brought enough money to live a year without panicking. The condo in Yorkville turned out to be as wonderful as I had hoped. The weather was warm and sunny so I just walked around getting reacquainted with the city, meeting friends for lunch, seeing the sights and playing tourist. Obviously my therapy with Dr. Young put me in a good place and the medication I was taking was doing the world of good. Susan Young had given me the name of a therapist in Toronto who I called and began seeing. I didn't even try and set up a business meeting for about a month. I was determined not to fall back into the pattern of putting pressure on myself or doubting my worth unless I had a job. It was about as easy for me as threading a needle with gloves on – but I made myself do it.

Culturally, Toronto is an incredible city, After Broadway and London's West End – Toronto has the most active and exciting theater scene in the world. Busloads of Americans arrive every day to see first run musicals and dramas. They come from Cleveland, Detroit, Chicago and Buffalo, etc. I had season tickets to the Toronto Symphony – a first class musical group. It was a great way to force you out of the house especially during the win- ter... even when it snowed. The city has great museums and art galleries. It's a very cosmopolitan town. Finally it was time to call some people in the Canadian television industry and let them know I was there for good. Although I still had my condo in Palm Springs I never wanted to go back to the States to live. I put the condo up for sale and sold it in six months. The reaction of the Canadian networks and production people couldn't have been nicer. They were pleased that I had moved there and were cer- tain we'd do business together. Suddenly, my production credits meant something to programming executives. I was a valuable and known talent. "Doing business" in Canada was slightly dif- ferent than doing business in Hollywood. There are very few se- ries that originate in Canada. They just don't have the budgets for them. Most of the top-rated shows on Canadian TV are Amer- ican series with the exception of Hockey. This reality probably feeds into the feeling of 'not being able to do it was well as Amer- icans.' That insecurity is a difficult thing to overcome. Rather than create their own series most of the production companies are content to basi- cally act as bankers for U.S. companies and stu- dios. American companies that shoot in Canada have Canadian partners who get tax rebates and incentives from the Federal government. These companies make good money without risk- ing anything so why risk trying to be creative and produce their own shows and Movies of the Week? It's too bad because there are some very talented companies who don't get involved pro- ducing their own things or get projects going. Since I wasn't in a hurry I could wait until something 'interesting' came up.

A thing I noticed after moving to Canada is not only do they say 'nord' for north; "sud" for south "Aboot" for about, and "eh?" a lot. While I lived in the States it never occurred to me write unless I was being paid. If I was paid, I wrote. My lame excuse was always I had nothing to write about. No ideas. Well, when I moved up 'nord' I began trying to write plays, books and screen- plays for my own enjoyment. What ma joy it was to allow myself to just write.

Gordon Farr who still lived in Los Angeles was hired to do a series called "Boogies Diner" in Canada. The American pro- duction company need a Canadian to honcho the series to get all that 'free money' so they hired Gordy. He asked whether I wanted to do it with him and I was very hesitant. Did I really want to jump into producing a series that I wasn't sure about? Farr who hadn't been back in Toronto since he left in the late 60s put a full course press on me. He flew up and we put a writing staff to- gether. The two Americans who ran the production company had lousy repu- tations. Everyone said they were untrustworthy swines. Turned out they were worse than that. When we met they didn't like me and the feeling was mutual. The young actors were all Canadian except for J.J. Bullock who played their boss and jeopardy. He was great. Franklin-Waterman, made a deal with a local station in Hamilton, Ontario. Hamilton was a depressed steel town which had seen better days. It was a 45-minute drive from Toronto and was in a snow belt and becomes hazardous from November until April. Production started and F/W immedi- ately began second guessing everything Gordon and I wanted to do which included scripts, casting, music – you name it. I decided that I was too old to play F/W's games and quit the series mid- way during the schedule. The interesting thing was I didn't get angry or anxious about being out of work. Maybe I had licked my demons or at least fought them to a draw.

Now that I had some time for myself I began to really think about my life. Where I had been and where I wanted to go. It was time to find out who the hell Arnold Kane was. I sat down at my computer and began to write my history. My intention was to be totally honest and not hold back anything including my warts. It took me two full days to do, but here's what I wrote and sent to friends.

> *"My name is Arnold Kane and I thought I'd tell you about me or as much as know about me. Firstly, I am a seriously depressed personality and have been that way most of my life. I have just learned that about myself. I thought my periods of depression just happened. But, the reality is that I am usually depressed with periods of feeling good, happy, healthy and most importantly safe.*

When I was a young boy I overheard my mother say that she couldn't wait for the summer to come so that she could get rid of me. She was talking about sending me off to summer camp and her comments were obviously innocent and off-handed. Unfortunately, I was a sensitive kid and took her literally. My parents wanted to get rid of me! When I had a nervous breakdown at age nine, I was returning from a dog show that neighbors took me to and went I entered my house it was empty. No one was home. I panicked. My parents finally had gotten 'rid of me' or more to the point left me alone for good. I guess I never forgot those two incidents. Oh, later I made fun of them, hell they didn't mean anything. Yes they did!

An important turning point in my childhood was when I was about twelve and my parents sent me off to visit old neighbors who had moved to Dover, Delaware. I remember being put on the train and crying all the way to Dover. Once again I was being sent away. I wasn't wanted. They didn't love me.

Fortunately, the Kugler family were fabulous people and welcomed me and made me part of their family. For one month I felt totally loved, secure and safe. I, also, got a look at how a family really behaved and acted towards each other. When Mr. Kugler came home at night we sat around and played games and he wanted to know something new that we all had learned that day. I usually sat mute – this being so alien to me but with their encouragement I finally began to participate. We were a family and I loved every minute of my four weeks there. I knew that the Kane family was not a place that I felt safe and happy in. It wasn't my parent's fault. I honestly believe they tried to do a good job with their two sons but I just wasn't enough for me. I began to distance myself from them and I guess my past. It wasn't a place of joy or happiness for Arnold. I had grown up frightened, scared and feeling unsafe. If I couldn't 'trust' my parents who could I trust?

So, I built a large thick wall around myself. I had to protect myself from being hurt anymore. If you don't trust people to take care of you or really care about you – you won't be let down.

You won't be disappointed. And, I guess that the way I lived my life all, these years.

When I started working in television I finally felt useful and secure. I had a purpose in life. I was good at something and turned my work into the most import-ant part of my life. I could create 'a family' in the work environment. It became a favorite saying of mine..." That my show and co-workers were my family." – that's how desperately I need family. Of course, when I wasn't work-ing I was miserable again. I felt inadequate, discour-aged, terrified and dejected because I had nobody to fall back on or feel secure with. I was frightened and didn't know why. So a pattern formed. I created a life-style, working meant happiness and approval. Life has meaning. Not working uncertainty, rejection and inad-equacy. I kept swinging back and forth, feeling secure and then feeling rejected. Feeling exhilarated one month and total gloom the next. Since I didn't allow anyone to break through my self-imposed wall of defenses I was stuck with myself and trying to cope with these dreadful feelings. No one was allowed to get too close because if I let my guard down they could hurt me. I would become that little, frightened boy again.

I have always made a big thing about helping others. I would spend more time and effort trying to get people – strangers many times – work. I would get furious when successful friends didn't lift a finger to help anyone. What I didn't realize until recently was that feeling

I'd get from helping somebody – that high – had little to do with that person. If somebody helped that person I was calling about was really

ARNOLD. I had value. People cared about me and listened to my opinions...they put themselves out for me. It was my sick way of getting approval. They did this 'favor' for me therefore they must like and love me. That 'needy' person I was trying to help was a substitute for me. I was praying that a friend would come along in those moments when I felt such despair and "help" me get a job. Put themselves out for me. IT WAS ALL ABOUT ME!!!!

It's amazing that for fifty-nine years I have lived in my body being totally discouraged and inadequate. Wanting to be loved, wanting to love but feeling too unsafe to really go for it. I hope I can try from now on. I can't take refuge in myself any longer. It doesn't work. I hope you will have patience with me as I start this journey. If you see me falling back into familiar patterns or tricks – call me on it. It's time I let that frightened boy out. It's time for me to grow up. Wow, this is hard."

Just the act of writing this was an epiphany of sorts. I knew I could never go back to being the person I was describing in the letter. As you can tell it was written ungrammatically with punc- tuation and spelling mistakes – almost like free association. That's exactly what I had done on the computer – free associate. Let my mind go without trying to structure anything. Once I con- nected all the dots I had been aware of at various times but never put together. It felt like a giant weight had been lifted from my shoulders. I sent this letter to every friend of mine to help them understand "why". I, also, knew there was no turning back – that I had crossed into a new life. A life I couldn't wait to run with. (But, boy, I also realized what a sick fucker I had been.)

The winter had been fairly mild but I still missed and craved the sun. I decided to take a week off and go to Club Med in Can- cun, Mexico. I had never before gone away on a vacation alone before. I'm not one of those dudes who makes friends that easily when surrounded by strangers. Club Meds are usually filled with young people wearing thong bikinis and I was approaching my 60th birthday. If I saw a 30-inch waist all over it would make me bonkers. I could show them a 30-inch neck. I decided to give it a shot. The worst thing that could happen was that I would get a good suntan, or be eaten by a shark. Club Med turned out to be a wonderful vacation. The people were friendly and the girls sexy. The food was unbelievable and the sun just what I needed.

I hated it when the week was up. An interesting thing happened at a night-time party at the end of the week.

There was this very attractive, tall, blonde girl that I had noticed around the pool. I was immediately drawn to her but didn't know why? There were lots of other really sexy women all over the place but something about her was special. One evening I went over the bar and began talking to her (the old Woody Allen nebbish routine) and made her promise not to hit me if I talked to her. It worked. She laughed and didn't slug me once. She was delightful and then I realized why I had noticed her. She looked a lot like my old girlfriend Hallie Stich who I hadn't thought of in years. It was spooky. Nothing happened between us but I found it interesting that someone who looked like Hallie could still excite me.

When I returned to Toronto they were in the middle of a blizzard. I had to wait over three hours to get transportation from the airport. Normally that would have made me a 'crazy' person but the 'new' me just stood waiting like everyone else. For Christ- mas Shelley and David Peterson invited me to their new horse farm outside the city to spend the holiday with their extended family. They had just bought the place and in the snow it looked like a picture postcard. Without doubt the Petersons were gra- cious, warm people who made me feel like I was part of their family. It was a lovely holiday.

Simon Muntner an old friend from the States and a really good writer has moved up to Toronto to find work. Simon was another one of us "grays" who had to go north to earn a living even though he had won an Emmy for a MASH he wrote. He and I came up with a television idea for a family series which I took to YTV the folks who loved "DOG HOUSE." We pitched 'JESSIE" to them which they really liked. It was the story of a family – hus- band, wife daughter, son and a cat named "Jessie." Cats, as you know, can be found anywhere unlike dogs. They can hang out on top of a bookshelf, under a chair, etc. That gave us very unu- sual angles to use in shooting the series. Also, "Jessie" commented on what the silly human beings doing. WE created an attitude for her and gave her a Southern accent, which seemed to play well with her sarcastic 'voice'. We handed the script in and YTV couldn't have been happier. WE pointed out that we couldn't shoot the series like a normal multi-camera com- edy because cats can't be trained unlike dogs. It had to be shot like a movie and we promised that the audience would get used to the process. The deal I had made with YTV was there was to be no pilot. If they liked the script they had to order an entire year's series. It was our way or no show. Sadly, YTV was too nervous to commit all that money on a new technique and finally passed. Simon and I were paid very, very well for our script and I still think Jessie was a great idea for a show.

Okay, strange coincidence time! Out of the blue I got a call from Carlinda Agrella in Arizona where she had moved. Wed hadn't talked in a while and bullshitting she asked me if I was seeing anyone seriously? I told her 'no'. She then said the magic words, "Why don't you call Hallie?" I told her to forget it. Hallie was old news and I hadn't spoken to her in twelve years. Carly wouldn't let up. She said that Hallie always asked about me. I kept telling her to get off my case. Carly yelled that I shouldn't be a stub- born asshole and give her a call. We hung up but a few days later I remembered my reaction to that girl at Club Med so I figured what the hell. Carlinda had given me Hallie's home num- ber in

Louisiana where she had moved. Figuring what the hell I called the number and left a message on her answering machine. I felt like a 16-year old kids calling a girl for a first date. She called back later that night and as soon as I heard her voice I began to smile. Even though twelve years had passed we picked up like we'd talked yesterday. After some light chitchat we warmed up and brought each other to date in our lives. She was now head of promotion for a large Insurance Underwriting Company in the south. We talked for about an hour which is pretty remarkable because I hate talking on the phone. Over the next several weeks we talked regularly and looked forward to those calls. I had decided to throw myself a 60th Birthday party at my condo and invited Hallie to fly up for it. She said she'd love to come and booked herself a flight from New Orleans. Turns out she lived in Covington, Louisiana about a forty-five minute drive from the 'Big Easy.' I had invited all my friends to the party and all accepted except for Larry and Laurel Dane who were flying to Las Vegas to get married and Shelley and David Peterson who were fox hunting in Ireland. I was very nervous about the reaction my Ca- nadian friends would have to Hallie. I had a big sign, "Welcome Hallie" printed which I hung over my fireplace. I picked her up at the airport, gave her a bouquet of flowers and the bill for them and we drove to my place. She hadn't changed one bit. We sat and talked, both of us nervous as two teenagers. After a couple of glasses of wine we made love. It was like we'd never been apart. We spent every waking hour together – something I had never been able to do with a woman. We held hands and talked and walked and couldn't get enough of each other. It was like a schmaltzy movie of two lovers reuniting. The birthday party was a big hit and everyone adored Hallie.

Guess my friends knew something important was happening. When she flew back on Sunday, it was understood that she was going to come back of- ten to visit. I flew her up a few times and she even drove up once to surprise me. We were in love and I finally realized that I was sixty-years old and it was time to stop being afraid of my feelings. I asked Hallie to marry me, something I thought I'd never do with someone. I never felt better letting myself become vulnerable and allow a woman into the deepest part of my soul. She con- fessed that that she had waited for me to ask her ever since we met at Warner Brothers and she agreed to become my wife.

My friends were thrilled with the news and the next time she flew up there were wall-to-wall parties to celebrate our en- gage- ment. We decided that I would fly to Covington and get mar- ried at her parent's home.

CHAPTER TWENTY-FIVE

Y'ALL COME BACK YA HEAR

I FLEW INTO NEW ORLEANS ON SEPTEMBER 28 1995 AND was met at the airport by Hallie an Carlinda – who I had chosen as my Best Man We drove to Covington and on the way I saw sign alongside the highway, "Cowboys for Jesus". I made Hallie stop the car and I took the sign – which I still have in my office. This Yankee was obviously gonna have a helluva time in Louisiana. I thought of the old joke, "A Jewish guy gets off a bus in Louisiana and asks, 'where do the Jews hang out? The answer is, "See that tree!" We were married the next day at her parent's home. Bob and Nancy Tefft turned out to be wonderful people and great in- laws.

Actually they had never met Hallie's second husband. Her brother and sister-in-law flew I for the wedding from California. The only things I insisted on was this was not going to be a reli- gious ceremony – a Justice of the Peace would do just fine. Bob and Nancy invited all their friends from Tchefuncta Country Club to the wedding. A few co-workers of Hallie's showed up, also. I didn't have to be introduced to the Justice of the Peace...I spotted him right away. He happened to be Bob's barber- so I was being married to a hyphenate – barber/justice. I looked around and saw a middle-aged guy in a crew cut, blue suit, brown shoes and white socks. I knew – 'this must be the guy'. After I paid him he asked us what sort of service we wanted? I told him, "a fast one!" He didn't quite understand and I explained: "do you? Do you? I now pronounced you man and wife" That's it. "Well, golly, okay." The ceremony started. Carlinda was besides me as best man and the Tefft's were standing next to Hallie. "Do you Arnold take Hallie to be your lawfully wedded wife...?" I did a great comedy pause and said, "Can I get back to you on that?" Everybody gasped. Hallie and Carlinda elbowed m in the ribs and I finally said, "Oh, okay." Before he could even get out, "Do you Hallie...?" she yelled out "Yes!" By then the Justice was white as a sheet (lousy pun for Louisiana)— "Well, I guess you're man and wife. You may kiss the bride." I kissed Carlinda, of course and we all laughed. The rest of the guests just stared and wanted to know when the wedding was going to start.

So, on Saturday, September 29, 1995 I got married. We took pictures, drank champagne, shook a lot of hands and kissed a few cheeks. When things 'calmed down' I started kidding Hallie in front of everyone. I told them that she had wanted a wedding cake with a bride, groom and divorce lawyer on top...that she was going to wear curlers to the wedding so she's look good for the divorceetc. The guest finally realized that we were just hav- ing fun and the rest of the night was as beautiful as my bride. I thanked Carly for flying in and told her she was the best best man I had ever had. I flew back to Toronto on Monday and Hallie went back to work. Our marriage consisted of talking on the phone every night or Hallie coming up for weekends or me driving down to Louisiana for short periods of time. It was not very romantic or satisfying for either of us. Long distance marriages don't work. I decided to move down to Covington around Christmas. I could write anyplace and it was too impractical. I went through a round of good-byes with all my Canadian friends. Leaving Toronto was very sad because it had been a very important part of my getting my life together. I packed up my car and headed down to Louisiana and officially changed my name to "Bubba." The truth is a 'Yankee' with any creativity and sensitivity trying to live in the 'deep south' has as much chance as Donald Trump does getting into MENSA.

Sometime between Christmas and New Years we had a big party at Hallie's house for all of Gilsbar so that her co-workers and bosses could meet this guy she married. It was a huge success and everyone seemed happy for us. When the holidays were over, things got back to normal. Hallie worked and I took an office across the road from her home. By the time my wife got back from work and feeding her horses I had made dinner for us. We'd just sit around, relax and talk about our day...kinda like the Sopranos.

Living in the South was quite an experience for me. The only thing I was familiar with was fried chicken. I'd like to share a few things I learned about Dixie and Southerners. I do this as a public service for all normal human beings:

When pulling up to a truck stop and seeing someone who is ill-kempt, scraggly, unshaven with a pot-belly hanging over baggy jeans, a pair of scuffed boots, cigarette in one hand and a can of Bud in the other wearing a stained John Deere cap on their head – you are looking at a real-live Southerner. Unfortunately the men don't look any better.

Southerners say 'damn' a lot. "My damn kid"..."Damn Com- mie Democrats"..."Damn that was a mighty fine chicken- fried steak"..."Did you see those damn hooters on her?"

Southern parents don't give their children real names – just initials. No one is named Bill, John, Mary or Ellen – just RB, TD, AC and the ever popular F.U.

Southerners are famous for their charm and friendliness. And, Lord, they do love to talk. You won't understand a word they're saying but that doesn't matter. They're always happy to welcome you to their home. "Pull up a damn rocker and set a damn spell". If they don't have a spare rocker you can always pull up a damn hound dog and set a spell. They love to party. Beer is the preferred drink most of the time. And, not some expensive damn foreign or de- signer beer. No siree, good old American brewskies are just fine, don't ya know. On special occasions folks might sip some Jack Daniels neat or even a mint julep – but they'd have to be celebrating something real damn special – somethin' where you'd wear a cummerbund with your coveralls. If you're goin' visitin' proper etiquette demands you bring a jug of wine to your hosts—a screw top is ac- ceptable.

Southerners love to hunt. They also wear camou- flage out- fits all the damn time. They wear it around the house, to work, to school, to Church and some are even buried in it. Camouflage is considered stylish and chic. I even saw one newborn in a camouflage diaper. Instead of a dam silver spoon in its mouth, it had a silver duck call. And don't make the mistake of talking about 'poor Bambi' to these good cit- izens. The only Bambi they know is the tramp cheerleader who's doing the entire High School football team.

I could go on and on - in fact I did in my book "IF THE SOUTH RISES AGAIN It'll BE OVER MY DEAD BODY."

Which I wrote after I left Louisiana.

Work-wise I was still writing some scripts for Canadian television which kept me busy and some damn grits on the table. I also began writing other projects which I had not tried before. Like a suspense murder/mystery about a serial killer in New Orleans, two plays and a book. I was having a ball. The Times-Picayune newspaper wrote an article about me. It was very complimentary an made me an import man with my in-laws. There's something to be said about being a big fish in a little pond. A few theaters were interested in my plays and a wonderful professor Andrew Horton who taught writing at Loyola University called and asked if I would lecture to his writing classes. I gladly took him up on his offer. Horton and his wife became friends with us.

My marriage was going along fine although Hallie's bosses at Gilsbar kept giving her more and more to do at the office. Despite this marriage seemed to really agree with me. When Hallie and I were hanging out together it really was excellent. Hanging out with my wife, fixing the house up, taking long drives and going out to dinner or just listening to music couldn't have been better. The one thing I learned quickly was that you cannot sit outside in Louisiana. The state is famous for its large man- eating, vicious bugs. Louisiana is below sea level – it's swampy which makes bugs very happy but not human beings. These bugs are huge and gigantic. The Japanese could have made a Godzilla film about them. As time went on Gilsbar kept piling work on my wife's shoulders which really began cutting into our time together. It got soooo bad I didn't see her for days at a time. Be- fore I knew it our first Anniversary was coming up and I went to a local jeweler in town and had him create a ring for her. I also booked us into the Grand Hotel in Alabama which is a famous, old landmark right on Mobil Bay.

It was a terrific week and we need the bonding and re- charging our batteries. When I gave her the ring she cried and asked if I was as happy as she was? I told her 'yes' but that I wished she didn't have to work so hard. Gilsbar had her working every night which made me crazy. She'd come home have a little dinner and literally fall asleep at her desk. The she'd get up and work for hours. She probably got two hours sleep a night and I told her it had to stop. Her bosses were taking advantage of her and it was hurting our marriage. I didn't move to Louisiana to be alone! Hallie promised to talk to them but she never did.

During the year Gordon Farr came to visit and we played some golf. Soon after he left Larry and Laurel Dane flew down from Toronto for a weekend. We ate ourselves crazy and did lots of sightseeing. Hallie could sometimes join us for dinner. I hadn't realized how much I missed my old friends. After our second Christmas together things began to unravel. She started working even crazier hours and often on weekends. Shit, I was really get- ting lonely. I explained again that I didn't move thousands of miles to be alone. It was obvious she had become a workaholic and even though I loved her this couldn't continue. I loved everything about her – her smell, her humor, her humanity...just her – but we couldn't continue the way we were. I was going to have to leave. Before I did, I received a call from the writing de- partment at LSU who wanted to hire me as a teacher. As much as I would have loved doing it I had to pass. Hallie asked that I make up a story for her parents saying I got this fabulous job offer in California that I couldn't turn down.

Before I leave the swamp called Louisiana you have to hear this real story. It was during the Bill Clinton/Bob Dole Presidential campaign. They were also electing a Senator at the same time. David Duke – the former head of the KKK and the Nazi party was running for Senator. I'd see him on the side of the road wearing a white sheet waving to cars and potential voters. No shit. I decided to call Duke whose number was in the phone book. He answered and I told him we had to get together. He gave me directions – he was about ten minutes from our house. I drove to his house in lovely area – there were David Duke signs all over the lawn. I pulled up and started walking up his driveway when I noticed six pick-ups from Utah, Idaho and Washington parked near his garage. Suddenly guys pile out of his front door and I had to stop myself from laughing.

They were obviously members of the militia – big guys with more tattoos than teeth! One yelled out, "Who you, boy?" I explained who I was and that I had an appointment with Hitler---- uh, I mean David Duke. They grinned their tooth at me and in- vited me in. Duke was doing a radio interview in his kitchen and when I entered he waved me to a chair opposite him. Duke is a handsome man who has had more plastic surgeries on his face than any Hollywood starlet. He finished his radio interview and asked what he could do for me? After a deep breath I said to him that he didn't really believe the bullshit he said and that he was a fucking nutcase! His mouth popped open and his bodyguards started towards me. I thought I was history. Duke then began to laugh and everyone relaxed a bit. We had coffee together and I kept baiting him as a stupid bigot and he should be ashamed of himself. I was enjoying myself and after an hour he suggested that we should do a radio talk show together. We could argue about everything under the sun. He'd be the conservative voice and I would be the liberal 'commie' spokesman. I told David that no sponsor would buy the idea and if we did I would kick his dumb ass all over the place. We finally broke up our meeting but not before he asked me to please take some of his, "Duke for Sena- tor "posters. I have one in my office right next to "Cowboys for Jesus."

Good riddance to Louisiana.

CHAPTER TWENTY-SIX

THE BACK NINE

AS EVERY GOLFER KNOWS A ROUND OF GOLF CONSISTS of 2 nines – the front and the back. It doesn't matter how good you play the first nine holes. The key is to play the last nine equally good or better. You want to finish strong and remain focused. How about that for a metaphor for living? As I play the back nine of my life, I'm determined not to 4 putt or shank any balls. Will this writer's cleverness ever stop?

When I hit New Mexico and saw the purple and pink mountains I took my first deep breath since leaving Louisiana. I smiled because I was going home to Palm Springs. When I hit the California border I was as happy as a clam. Did you ever wonder about that phrase 'happy as a clam'? Did you ever see a happy clam? I mean, how do you know if they're happy? Do they smile, wink, laugh or giggle? Next time I order clams on the half shell I'm gonna listen for any chortling.

I rented a furnished condo at The Greenhouse West – where I had lived before. I didn't want to own anything again. I was starting life over again for the third time. Hallie and I got di- vorced. I stayed at the Greenhouse West until 2003. In that year I listened to all my friends and bought a home in Cathedral City which I still live in. Some things in the desert never change. Whenever I look at the mountains surrounding us I still get goose bumps. It's so darn beautiful when I'm playing golf in my shorts and look up at the snow-covered mountains – just like a picture postcard.

My new home is five minutes by golf cart from Mission Hills Country Club which I joined again. I had been a member since 1986 except for the Toronto and 'Big Easy" trips. Yes, I drive my own golf cart and it's quite a sight seeing me doing 'wheelies' along Gerald Ford Drive. My house is great for entertaining which I do frequently. My friends love to come over for my great Jambalaya, corn bread and sweet potato pie dinners. Not bad for a kid who grew up in Brooklyn and never ate anything without ketchup on it. A lot has happened since my move and all of it good. I rejoined Mission Hills and they welcomed me back with my open wallet. Now owners had taken over while I was away and the new General Manager, Tom Catanzarite, asked if I could come up with something to get the members to start to hang around at night having dinner and drinks. I suggested that I pro- duce musical evenings each month at MHCC and they became a big hit and sold out. I hired local talent or performers from Las Vegas. I did that for ten years which kept my producing chops alive. The shows had gotten so popular that and with good press I was doing them at 7 country clubs in the desert. It became too much work and I just cut it back to MHCC.

The Kraft Nabisco LPGA golf tournament – formally the Dinah Shore Tourney began to invite me to play in the Pro-Am each April. I played in 11 of them. The silly fools considered me a 'half- ass local celebrity of some sort. It was fun and I had gotten to know many of the tour players well. I, also, knew lots of the real celebrity that played having worked with many of them during my career: Jaime Farr, Alice Cooper, Peter Marshall, Andy Williams, Johnny Mathis, Norm Crosby, Tommy Smothers. Ceech Marin, Jack Jones, Susan Anton, Harry Conic, Smokey Robinson and Michael Bolton to name a few. It was always a fun-filled week filled with parties, good food and plenty of drink. I won't discuss my golf game because I don't want to depress myself.

I'm a regular at the McCallum Theater in Palm Desert a great place to see shows. I also try to catch all local community theater presentations. Sleepy old Palm Springs had grown up big time and even has a famous Film Festival each year. I play golf each week with my golfing buddies – Steve Jacobson, Jim Noel, Ron Cuvier, David Manovitch, Isao Sumac, Bob Guss, John Sanders, and a host of other hustlers who kick my butt. One of the most interesting things about my life is that I have no desire or interest in ever writing for television again. Been there/done that.

Physically, I've been pretty lucky. This year I will be 85 years old. I did have a stroke a few years ago and was pretty sick.

They put a pacemaker in and it took me a while to get strong again. Went to a small Gym in Palm desert, "Zacks Per- sonal Fitness" and Zack and Jason got me healthy again. I, still go to

Zack's twice a week. I rarely drive into Los Angeles any- more even though Ron Cukier has a brownstone in Beverly Hills.

L.A. is no longer the charming city it was when I lived there. It's noisy, dirty and angry. Who needs it.

I lost my darling friends Bruce Johnson, Bill D'Angelo and Sam Denoff recently. They were great and loyal chums and I miss them a lot. I guess when we reach our age these things are to be expected. I check the orbits every day to find out if I should put both shoes on. Sometime in the 2000's I got a strange call from Godon Farr who now lives in Toronto and obviously had just joined a twelve step program. His call was to apologize for some of the shitty things he had done to me in the past and to ask for my forgiveness. Like I said earlier, our partnership was like a marriage – you take the good with the bad. We had quite a run together and I told Gordy that if apologizing made him feel better so be it. We still talk a lot and I see him when he comes down in the winter to get some sun. My Toronto connection is more than just Farr. I visit Toronto frequently to see my dear friends Larry and Laurel Dane who live in Niagara-on-the-Lake which is a won- derful town. They, also, come down to Palm Springs each year during the winter. I love them both.

I have not been lazy. I have written and published a book about the south, 'IF THE SOUTH RISES AGAIN IT'LL BE OVER MY DEAD BODY" which sold nicely. Western Connecticut State University hired me to mentor MFA writing students which I did for two years. We did it over the Internet. I've written a few screenplays which were optioned but not bought. Soon after I came back to the desert I read about an organization called "Playwright's Circle" which gave new playwrights an opportunity to have their plays produced. I sat down and wrote, SHARING A LIFE" which won the first prize and was produced for one week at a local theater. There was a cash award for the winning playwright and I won the 2000 Playwright's Circle Award. I felt pretty damn good about the whole thing. Next, I wrote 'LOVE IS A 4 LETTER WORD" which was a comedy with music and that played in Palm Spring's Canyon Playhouse. If I'm losing some gray matter in my brain you'd never know it.

CHAPTER TWENTY-SEVEN
WHAT'S NEXT

THE THING I LEARNED FROM MY FAILED MARRIAGE was that I en- joyed sharing my life with someone I can love. Living alone no longer held any attraction for me.

Remember the name SALLY BARTH? She was the girl I had a deep relationship with in the late 50's and 60's. Sally had worked as an editor at Vogue Magazine at the time and I was producing Pantomime Quiz. We could just never get it together. She had gotten married and had a daughter named Allison. Over forty years had gone by when I got home from playing golf and the message light was blinking on my telephone machine. I have already mentioned my antipathy with phones – hate the suckers. Normally, I would quickly listen to the message or sometimes just delete the message. With robo-calls today, that was very usual for me. Must have been in a good mood because I listened to the message. "Hi, Arnold, this is Sally " I couldn't make out the last name but kept listening to the message a few times until I figured out the voice was saying "Barth." "I would love to talk to you." Sally Barth was calling me? She left a number and I called her back. At that moment she happened to be in Bend, Oregon but was heading back to her home in La Jolla, California the next day. How weird was that? We talked briefly and brought each other up on our lives. She was a widow after a long, happy mar- riage. Her daughter was now a graphic artist living in NYC. Sally is a grandmother. She also owned a thriving tee-shirt business with a factory in Bend, Oregon. Turns out, Sally does the designs on the shirts and her partner, Sondra, is the business maven. The business was doing really well. I always loved Sally' creativ- ity even when we were kids together. She returned to San Diego and we decided that I should drive down the next day to see her.

I drove down although I was a little anxious. It was over forty years since we'd seen each other.

When we met it was like we had never been apart. It was one of those magical moments when two people get together af- ter ages and come together and like it was like they were never apart. Was it love? Probably! One smart due once said you never get over your first love. Sally was mine and it looked like nothing had changed. We started seeing each other as much as possible. She'd drive up from San Diego every few days. We finally decided that she should move up to my new house and be together. Thanks God. She is the best thing to ever happen to me and we love each other totally. She's funny, bright and loyal and brought peace to my soul. We adopted two cats. 'Blacky' and 'Goldie' who run my life. I had never had animals in my life be- fore. I still play golf a few times a week and Sally's started paint- ing again. I'm her biggest fan. We have been together for ten years and they are the best I ever lived. A few years ago, after playing golf and not drinking enough water in the heat down here I came home and collapsed on the kitchen floor splitting my head open. I got a concussion and had to go the hospital. I was in bad shape for about a month. With the help of Sally and Jim Noel I finally got better. That's why I go to the gym twice a week now. No problems since.

Sally and I have both been creative and I'm writing more and better than I ever did. I've written 3 books, 'HOW THE ANIMALS SAVED CHRISTMAS', 'MY METERORIC RISE TO OBSCURITY' and THE FREAKY WORLD OF SHOW

BUSINESS.' I won the 'ONE ACT COMEDY PLAY FESTIVAL" in Durango, Colorado for "THAT'S AMORE." The 'FILMAKER WORLD FESTIVAL' for my movie 'NOW AND FOREVER'. My other plays and screenplays, "Sharing A life, Vengeance, The Queen Must Die, Jack The Ripper Is Alive & Well in New Orleans, Marriage Can Be Hazardous to Your Health, Kimmelman, What Are Friends For? Etc., have also won awards.

None of this could have happened without Sally Barth Gromis in my Life. Thanks, baby.